First published in 2005 by Bardfield Press

Bardfield Press is an imprint of
Miles Kelly Publishing Ltd
Bardfield Centre, Great Bardfield,
Essex, CM7 4SL

British Library Cataloguing-in-Publication Data.
A catalogue record for this book is available from the British Library

ISBN 1-84236-583-5

2 4 6 8 10 9 7 5 3 1

Editorial Director: Belinda Gallagher

Project Manager: Lisa Clayden

Editorial Assistant: Amanda Askew

Production Manager: Estela Boulton

Designer: Helen Weller

Questions: Brian Williams

Cartoons: Mark Davis

Contact us by email:
info@mileskelly.net

Visit us on the web:
www.mileskelly.net

Printed in China

Contents

How to use this book

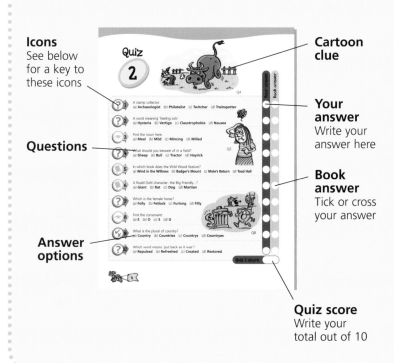

Icons
See below for a key to these icons

Questions

Answer options

Cartoon clue

Your answer
Write your answer here

Book answer
Tick or cross your answer

Quiz score
Write your total out of 10

Your book is split into four subject sections each with 28 quizzes, each quiz contains ten multiple-choice questions. There are six subject categories in each section for you to choose from. Simply write your answers in pencil in the answer panel. Turn to the answers at the back of the book to check your answers. Rub out your answers and try again! You can chart your progress by using the score sheets at the end of each section.

Homework Champions

Words and Writing

Key to subject icons

 Word meanings

 Books and stories

 Spellings

 Writing

 Grammar

 Sounds and rhymes

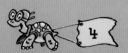

Words and Writing QUIZ

1

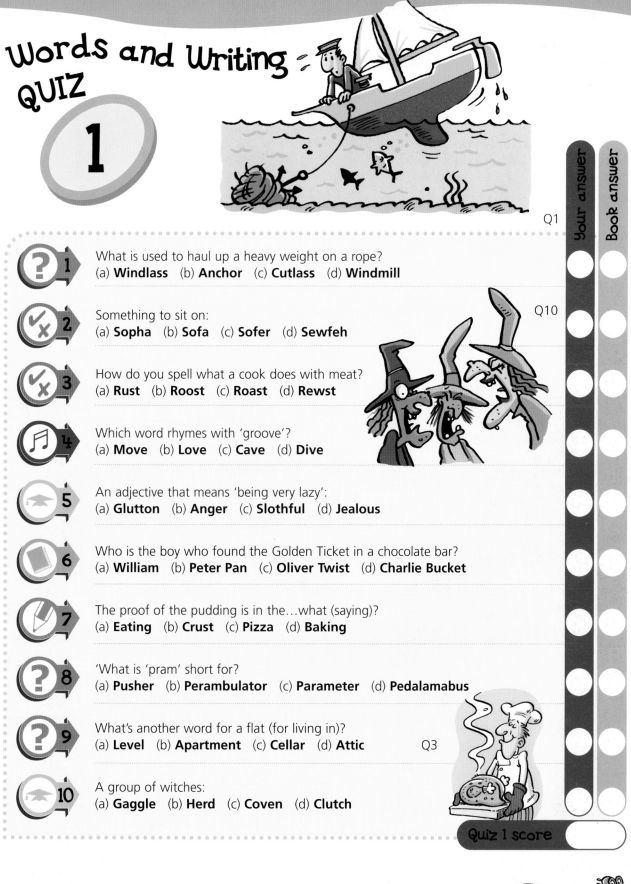

1 What is used to haul up a heavy weight on a rope?
(a) **Windlass** (b) **Anchor** (c) **Cutlass** (d) **Windmill**

2 Something to sit on:
(a) **Sopha** (b) **Sofa** (c) **Sofer** (d) **Sewfeh**

3 How do you spell what a cook does with meat?
(a) **Rust** (b) **Roost** (c) **Roast** (d) **Rewst**

4 Which word rhymes with 'groove'?
(a) **Move** (b) **Love** (c) **Cave** (d) **Dive**

5 An adjective that means 'being very lazy':
(a) **Glutton** (b) **Anger** (c) **Slothful** (d) **Jealous**

6 Who is the boy who found the Golden Ticket in a chocolate bar?
(a) **William** (b) **Peter Pan** (c) **Oliver Twist** (d) **Charlie Bucket**

7 The proof of the pudding is in the…what (saying)?
(a) **Eating** (b) **Crust** (c) **Pizza** (d) **Baking**

8 'What is 'pram' short for?
(a) **Pusher** (b) **Perambulator** (c) **Parameter** (d) **Pedalamabus**

9 What's another word for a flat (for living in)?
(a) **Level** (b) **Apartment** (c) **Cellar** (d) **Attic**

10 A group of witches:
(a) **Gaggle** (b) **Herd** (c) **Coven** (d) **Clutch**

Q10

Q3

Quiz 1 score

Words and Writing QUIZ

2

Q4

 1 A stamp collector:
(a) **Archaeologist**   (b) **Philatelist**   (c) **Twitcher**   (d) **Trainspotter**

 2 A word meaning 'feeling sick':
(a) **Hysteria**   (b) **Vertigo**   (c) **Claustrophobia**   (d) **Nausea**

3 Find the noun here:
(a) **Meal**   (b) **Mild**   (c) **Mincing**   (d) **Milled**

Q2

 4 What should you beware of in a field?
(a) **Sheep**   (b) **Bull**   (c) **Tractor**   (d) **Hayrick**

 5 In which book does the Wild Wood feature?
(a) **Wind in the Willows**   (b) **Badger's Mount**   (c) **Mole's Return**   (d) **Toad Hall**

6 A Roald Dahl character: the Big Friendly...?
(a) **Giant**   (b) **Rat**   (c) **Dog**   (d) **Martian**

 7 Which is the female horse?
(a) **Folly**   (b) **Fetlock**   (c) **Furlong**   (d) **Filly**

 8 Find the consonant:
(a) **E**   (b) **O**   (c) **S**   (d) **U**

Q8

 9 What is the plural of country?
(a) **Country**   (b) **Countries**   (c) **Countrys**   (d) **Countryes**

 10 Which word means 'put back as it was'?
(a) **Repulsed**   (b) **Refreshed**   (c) **Created**   (d) **Restored**

 Quiz 2 score

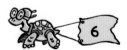

Words and Writing QUIZ

3

1 Which of these was a Russian writer?
(a) **Tolstoy**   (b) **Dickens**   (c) **Twain**   (d) **Burns**

Q3

2 Which is the adverb?
(a) **Bright**   (b) **Brightness**   (c) **Brightly**   (d) **Brighter**

3 A person looking on is a ... what?
(a) **Pedestrian**   (b) **Spectator**   (c) **Terrestrial**   (d) **Motorist**

4 A loud bang:
(a) **Examination**   (b) **Exhibition**   (c) **Explanation**   (d) **Explosion**

5 The plural of lesson is …what?
(a) **Lesson**   (b) **Lessones**   (c) **Lesson's**   (d) **Lessons**

6 Sarah was very happy, she was ... what?
(a) **Exasperated**   (b) **Exhausted**   (c) **Excited**   (d) **Ecstatic**

Q7

7 One goose, ten … what?
(a) **Gooses**   (b) **Geese**   (c) **Gice**   (d) **Geeses**

8 Complete this sentence to make sense: 'Coal fires are ...':
(a) **Good to eat**   (b) **Electric**   (c) **Hot**   (d) **Freezing**

9 What do you get in a shop after paying?
(a) **Recipe**   (b) **Receipt**   (c) **Record**   (d) **Remedy**

10 What does a plagiarist do?
(a) **Collect shells**   (b) **Lie on the beach**   (c) **Copy someone's work**
(d) **Tell lies**

Quiz 3 score

Words and Writing QUIZ

4

Q2

1 As ... as a lion (proverb):
(a) **Fat** (b) **Brave** (c) **Deaf** (d) **Silent**

2 Who wrote plays for the Globe Theatre?
(a) **Byron** (b) **Austen** (c) **Shakespeare** (d) **Ayckbourne**

3 Which isn't a punctuation mark?
(a) **Division sign** (b) **Full stop** (c) **Colon** (d) **Question Mark**

4 Fill in the missing word in the book title: The Worst ... :
(a) **Teacher** (b) **Goalkeeper** (c) **Astronaut** (d) **Witch**

5 Everything and everywhere:
(a) **Underground** (b) **Universe** (c) **Untidy** (d) **University**

Q9

6 What scared Little Miss Muffet?
(a) **Dragon** (b) **Spider** (c) **Toadstool** (d) **Witch**

7 Which of these is a preposition?
(a) **By** (b) **Moving** (c) **Clever** (d) **Tom**

8 Easy ... what (saying)?
(a) **Peasy** (b) **Greasy** (c) **Measly** (d) **Weesy**

9 Spell a word that means 'not very clever':
(a) **Stoopid** (b) **Stewpid** (c) **Stupid** (d) **Stupyd**

Q6

10 Which word rhymes with 'shiny'?
(a) **Tinny** (b) **Tiny** (c) **Slimy** (d) **Grimy**

Quiz 4 score

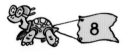

Words and Writing QUIZ

5

Q4

1 Which spelling is correct for the day of the week?
(a) **Toosday**   (b) **Towsday**   (c) **Tuesday**   (d) **Twosday**

Q10

2 A book full of names and addresses:
(a) **Journal**   (b) **Dictionary**   (c) **Directory**   (d) **Atlas**

3 Which is wrong here?
(a) **Ten dogs**   (b) **Four cats**   (c) **Ten beetle's**   (d) **Fifteen cars**

4 Which spelling is correct?
(a) **Hippopotamus**   (b) **Hypopotamus**   (c) **Hipopodamus**   (d) **Hipperpottamoos**

5 Who went to London with his cat?
(a) **Buttons**   (b) **Dick Whittington**   (c) **Aladdin**   (d) **Peter Pan**

6 Something to ride on:
(a) **Scooter**   (b) **Skipper**   (c) **Shopper**   (d) **Slipper**

Q6

7 Word meaning to bear flowers:
(a) **Sprout**   (b) **Grow**   (c) **Bloom**   (d) **Wilt**

8 Which of these is correct?
(a) **Sam's shoes**   (b) **Sams shoes**   (c) **Sams' shoe's**   (d) **Sammes' shoes'**

9 Which word is a noun here?
(a) **Run**   (b) **Tent**   (c) **Slowly**   (d) **Terrible**

10 Mythical animal, half human and half horse:
(a) **Centaur**   (b) **Sentaur**   (c) **Centore**   (d) **Scentaur**

Quiz 5 score

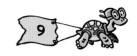

9

Words and Writing QUIZ

6

Q7

1 A word that means 'cross':
(a) **Distraught** (b) **Irate** (c) **Dejected** (d) **Baffled**

Q2

2 What we do on holiday:
(a) **Rellax** (b) **Relax** (c) **Reelacks** (d) **Rilacs**

3 The opposite of closed:
(a) **Tight** (b) **Open** (c) **Undressed** (d) **Shut**

4 Which of these would you find in the kitchen?
(a) **Spittoon** (b) **Spatula** (c) **Spade** (d) **Spreadsheet**

5 Which mark shows something belongs to someone?
(a) **Apostrophe** (b) **Full stop** (c) **Exclamation mark** (d) **Question Mark**

6 What's the correct short form for 'you are'?
(a) **You're** (b) **Your** (c) **Y'oure** (d) **Yo'are**

Q10

7 Which adjective goes best with 'elephant'?
(a) **Enormous** (b) **Tiny** (c) **Slimy** (d) **Green**

8 Which writer created Winnie the Pooh?
(a) **A.A. Milne** (b) **Richmal Crompton** (c) **Raymond Briggs** (d) **Roald Dahl**

9 Which marks show that someone is speaking?
(a) **!** (b) **"** (c) **?** (d) **^**

10 Which is the correct plural?
(a) **Slimy snail's** (b) **Slimys snails** (c) **Slimy snails** (d) **Slimeys snailes**

Quiz 6 score

Words and Writing QUIZ

7

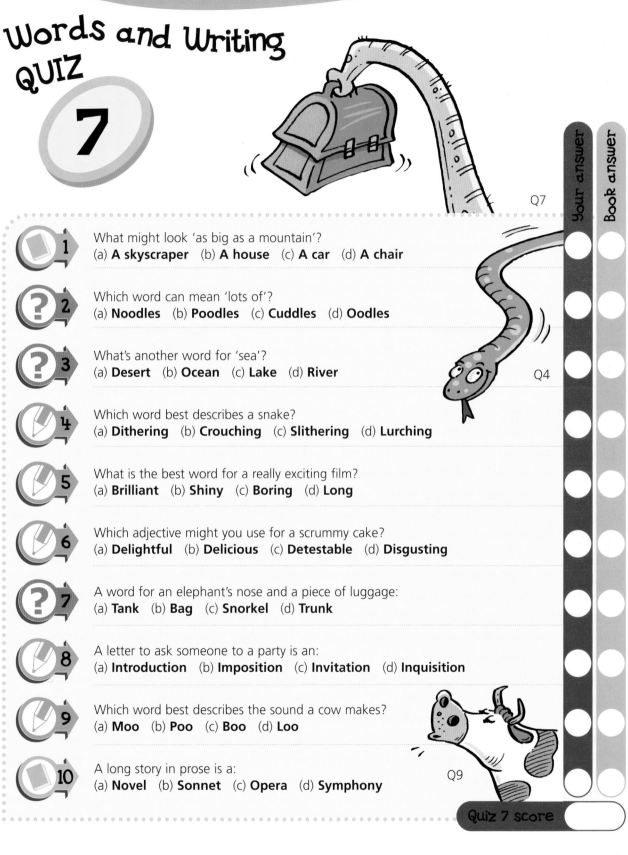

Q7

1 What might look 'as big as a mountain'?
(a) **A skyscraper** (b) **A house** (c) **A car** (d) **A chair**

2 Which word can mean 'lots of'?
(a) **Noodles** (b) **Poodles** (c) **Cuddles** (d) **Oodles**

3 What's another word for 'sea'?
(a) **Desert** (b) **Ocean** (c) **Lake** (d) **River**

Q4

4 Which word best describes a snake?
(a) **Dithering** (b) **Crouching** (c) **Slithering** (d) **Lurching**

5 What is the best word for a really exciting film?
(a) **Brilliant** (b) **Shiny** (c) **Boring** (d) **Long**

6 Which adjective might you use for a scrummy cake?
(a) **Delightful** (b) **Delicious** (c) **Detestable** (d) **Disgusting**

7 A word for an elephant's nose and a piece of luggage:
(a) **Tank** (b) **Bag** (c) **Snorkel** (d) **Trunk**

8 A letter to ask someone to a party is an:
(a) **Introduction** (b) **Imposition** (c) **Invitation** (d) **Inquisition**

9 Which word best describes the sound a cow makes?
(a) **Moo** (b) **Poo** (c) **Boo** (d) **Loo**

10 A long story in prose is a:
(a) **Novel** (b) **Sonnet** (c) **Opera** (d) **Symphony**

Q9

Quiz 7 score

Words and Writing QUIZ

8

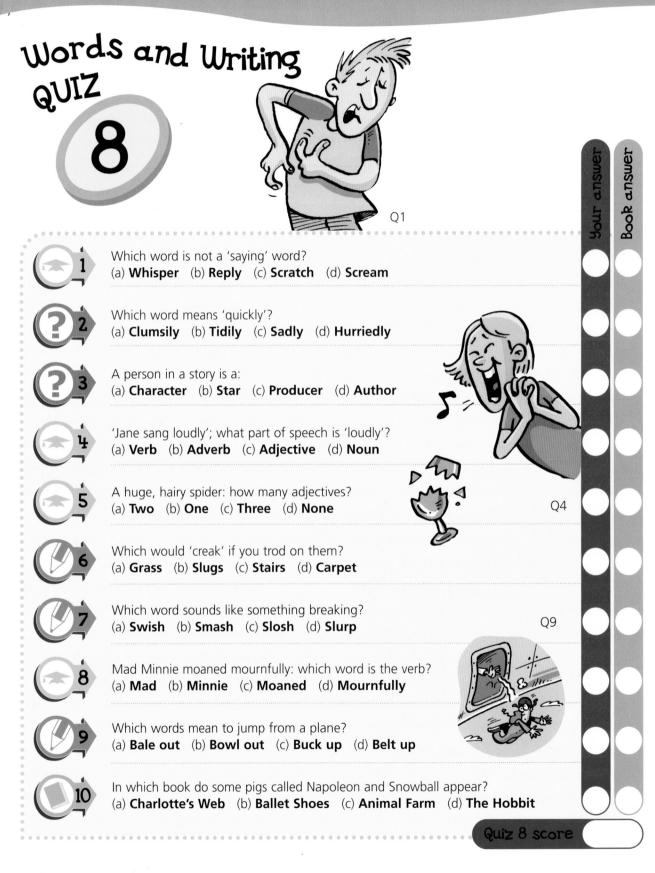

Q1

		Your answer	Book answer

1 Which word is not a 'saying' word?
(a) **Whisper**   (b) **Reply**   (c) **Scratch**   (d) **Scream**

2 Which word means 'quickly'?
(a) **Clumsily**   (b) **Tidily**   (c) **Sadly**   (d) **Hurriedly**

3 A person in a story is a:
(a) **Character**   (b) **Star**   (c) **Producer**   (d) **Author**

4 'Jane sang loudly'; what part of speech is 'loudly'?
(a) **Verb**   (b) **Adverb**   (c) **Adjective**   (d) **Noun**

5 A huge, hairy spider: how many adjectives?
(a) **Two**   (b) **One**   (c) **Three**   (d) **None**

Q4

6 Which would 'creak' if you trod on them?
(a) **Grass**   (b) **Slugs**   (c) **Stairs**   (d) **Carpet**

7 Which word sounds like something breaking?
(a) **Swish**   (b) **Smash**   (c) **Slosh**   (d) **Slurp**

Q9

8 Mad Minnie moaned mournfully: which word is the verb?
(a) **Mad**   (b) **Minnie**   (c) **Moaned**   (d) **Mournfully**

9 Which words mean to jump from a plane?
(a) **Bale out**   (b) **Bowl out**   (c) **Buck up**   (d) **Belt up**

10 In which book do some pigs called Napoleon and Snowball appear?
(a) **Charlotte's Web**   (b) **Ballet Shoes**   (c) **Animal Farm**   (d) **The Hobbit**

Quiz 8 score

Words and Writing
QUIZ

Q1

 1 What's not a way of saying goodbye?
(a) **Bye-bye**   (b) **So long**   (c) **See you**   (d) **Hi there**

 2 A place for storing hay:
(a) **Barn**   (b) **Burn**   (c) **Bairn**   (d) **Byre**

 3 A word that means 'not very big':
(a) **Slanted**   (b) **Stunted**   (c) **Static**   (d) **Sluggish**

Q6

 4 An old-fashioned pen:
(a) **Scroll**   (b) **Quill**   (c) **Quilt**   (d) **Parchment**

 5 Which prefix means big?
(a) **Mini-**   (b) **Mega-**   (c) **Milli-**   (d) **Micro-**

 6 A noisy piece of sports equipment:
(a) **Rocket**   (b) **Rabbit**   (c) **Racket**   (d) **Cracker**

 7 What often shows a new paragraph?
(a) **A space**   (b) **A full stop**   (c) **A new page**   (d) **A question mark**

 8 Which word means a group of wolves?
(a) **Herd**   (b) **Tribe**   (c) **Pack**   (d) **Flock**

 9 In the past tense, I eat becomes ... what?
(a) **I eated**   (b) **I ated**   (c) **I eat'**   (d) **I ate**

Q4

 10 What's the comparative of 'old'?
(a) **Older**   (b) **Ageing**   (c) **Elderly**   (d) **Oldest**

Quiz 9 score

Words and Writing QUIZ

10

Q3

1 Find the noun or 'naming word':
(a) **Hedge** (b) **High** (c) **Horrible** (d) **Hungry**

2 Which word must always have a capital letter?
(a) **Year** (b) **Day** (c) **Sunday** (d) **Month**

Q4

3 Which of these is a noun?
(a) **Sleepy** (b) **Sleep** (c) **Slept** (d) **Sleeping**

4 Which of these means a group of sheep?
(a) **Flock** (b) **Flick** (c) **Fleck** (d) **Flurry**

5 Spell the plural of toy:
(a) **Toy's** (b) **Toy** (c) **Toys** (d) **Toyes**

6 How do you spell the 1st month of the year?
(a) **Jangywerry** (b) **Janyuarry** (c) **Jannurry** (d) **January**

Q8

7 Which of these is the infinitive of the verb?
(a) **Doing** (b) **To do** (c) **Done** (d) **Did**

8 To lose hair or feathers:
(a) **Melt** (b) **Mint** (c) **Mope** (d) **Moult**

9 Find the pronoun:
(a) **Him** (b) **Hungry** (c) **Henry** (d) **House**

10 Which is the object of the sentence in 'I neatly caught the red ball'?
(a) **I** (b) **Kicked** (c) **Neatly** (d) **The red ball**

Quiz 10 score

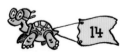

Words and Writing QUIZ

11

Q2

1 Which word here always needs a capital N?
(a) **Number** (b) **Nicholas** (c) **Night** (d) **Next**

Q6

2 C.S. Lewis created this magical land:
(a) **Scotia** (b) **Toyland** (c) **Narnia** (d) **Never Never Land**

3 A bird and to complain:
(a) **Whinge** (b) **Grumble** (c) **Moan** (d) **Grouse**

4 Where does a full stop go?
(a) **End of a sentence** (b) **Start of a sentence** (c) **Middle of a sentence**
(d) **End of a piece of work**

5 Which of these shows a person is speaking?
(a) **Quote marks** (b) **Capital Letters** (c) **Question Mark** (d) **Apostrophe**

6 What's the plural of tooth?
(a) **Tooths** (b) **Toothes** (c) **Tooth** (d) **Teeth**

7 Who is the popular writer?
(a) **Freda Wilson** (b) **Wilma Wilson** (c) **Jacqueline Wilson** (d) **Wendy Wilson**

8 Place where butter is made:
(a) **Dairy** (b) **Diary** (c) **Laundry** (d) **Dictionary**

9 A kind of fish-eating bird:
(a) **Oyster** (b) **Osprey** (c) **Ostrich** (d) **Ocelot**

Q9

10 Which is the verb here?
(a) **Slid** (b) **Slippery** (c) **Slipper** (d) **Slingshot**

Quiz 11 score

15

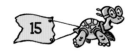

Words and Writing QUIZ

12

Q4

 1 Which word means a long chunk of time?
(a) **Episode** (b) **Epoch** (c) **Epistle** (d) **Epitaph**

Q5

 2 "HeyX" I shouted: what goes where the X is?
(a) **!** (b) **?** (c) **"** (d) **;**

 3 Which of these is a storybook cat?
(a) **Spot** (b) **Bill** (c) **Rupert** (d) **Mog**

 4 What's another word for 'fat'?
(a) **Stout** (b) **Stiff** (c) **Straight** (d) **Stuck-up**

 5 Kylie has a kitten; the kitten is ... who's?
(a) **Kylies** (b) **Kylies'** (c) **Kyliees** (d) **Kylie's**

 6 In which book do you start at Genesis?
(a) **Lord of the Rings** (b) **The Bible** (c) **Yellow Pages** (d) **Treasure Island**

 7 What part of speech is 'quickly' in 'He dressed quickly'?
(a) **A noun** (b) **Adverb** (c) **Verb** (d) **Preposition**

 8 Which missing letter or letters are shown by the apostrophe in 'It's raining'?
(a) **Was** (b) **i** (c) **o** (d) **might be**

Q10

 9 How do you spell the capital of Scotland?
(a) **Eddyinbur** (b) **Edinburk** (c) **Edinburgh** (d) **Eddinburg**

 10 What does claustrophobic mean?
(a) **Fear of heights** (b) **Fear of being shut in** (c) **Fear of clouds**
(d) **Fear of Santa Claus**

Quiz 12 score

Words and Writing QUIZ

13

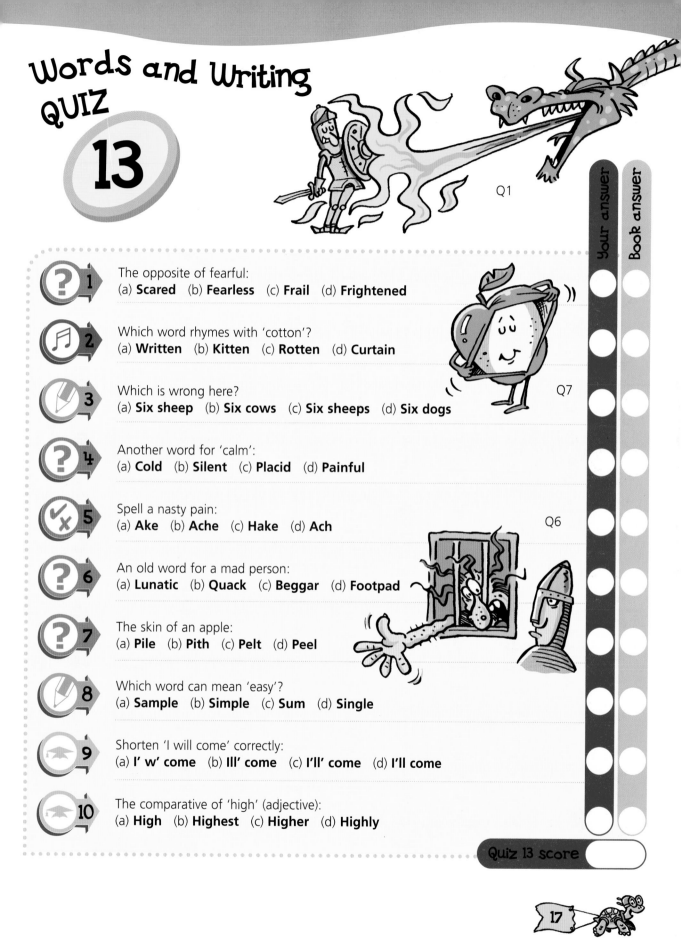

Q1

Your answer

Book answer

1 The opposite of fearful:
(a) **Scared** (b) **Fearless** (c) **Frail** (d) **Frightened**

2 Which word rhymes with 'cotton'?
(a) **Written** (b) **Kitten** (c) **Rotten** (d) **Curtain**

3 Which is wrong here?
(a) **Six sheep** (b) **Six cows** (c) **Six sheeps** (d) **Six dogs**

Q7

4 Another word for 'calm':
(a) **Cold** (b) **Silent** (c) **Placid** (d) **Painful**

5 Spell a nasty pain:
(a) **Ake** (b) **Ache** (c) **Hake** (d) **Ach**

Q6

6 An old word for a mad person:
(a) **Lunatic** (b) **Quack** (c) **Beggar** (d) **Footpad**

7 The skin of an apple:
(a) **Pile** (b) **Pith** (c) **Pelt** (d) **Peel**

8 Which word can mean 'easy'?
(a) **Sample** (b) **Simple** (c) **Sum** (d) **Single**

9 Shorten 'I will come' correctly:
(a) **I' w' come** (b) **Ill' come** (c) **I'll' come** (d) **I'll come**

10 The comparative of 'high' (adjective):
(a) **High** (b) **Highest** (c) **Higher** (d) **Highly**

Quiz 13 score

17

Words and Writing QUIZ

14

Q7

Q8

		Your answer	Book answer

1 Find the adverb here:
(a) **Slug**　(b) **Slow**　(c) **Slowness**　(d) **Slowly**

2 How many consonants in 'through'?
(a) **Five**　(b) **Two**　(c) **Seven**　(d) **None**

3 Which of these would not be a compliment?
(a) **Graceful**　(b) **Handsome**　(c) **Elegant**　(d) **Hideous**

4 What is a good word to describe peace and calm?
(a) **Serene**　(b) **Rowdy**　(c) **Sad**　(d) **Elegant**

5 A place of worship:
(a) **Mosk**　(b) **Mosque**　(c) **Mossk**　(d) **Music**

6 Which word could be a noun and a verb?
(a) **Choose**　(b) **Meat**　(c) **Selection**　(d) **Taste**

7 'The hat of Molly'– which is correct here?
(a) **Mollys hat**　(b) **'Mollys hat**　(c) **Mollys' hat**　(d) **Molly's hat**

8 Spell a word that means a sport:
(a) **Affleticks**　(b) **Afletics**　(c) **Atheletics**　(d) **Athletics**

9 Which is wrong here?
(a) **Six ships**　(b) **Seven Seas**　(c) **Four Buse's**　(d) **Two toys**

10 A word that describes a horse:
(a) **Equal**　(b) **Equine**　(c) **Equinox**　(d) **Equivalent**

Quiz 14 score

Words and Writing QUIZ

15

Q1

Your answer **Book answer**

1. Which word rhymes with 'pleasant'?
   (a) **Present**   (b) **Pleasing**   (c) **Pleasure**   (d) **Feather**

2. What did Jack and Jill go up?
   (a) **An escalator**   (b) **A hill**   (c) **A mountain**   (d) **A windy road**

3. Which is not a verb here?
   (a) **Swim**   (b) **Float**   (c) **Dive**   (d) **Pond**

   Q2

4. Opposite of 'honest':
   (a) **Dishonest**   (b) **Unhonest**   (c) **Mishonest**   (d) **Evil**

5. A verb and a carpenter's tool:
   (a) **See**   (b) **Saw**   (c) **Sew**   (d) **Sow**

6. Which spelling is correct here?
   (a) **Ellyfant**   (b) **Ellephant**   (c) **Elephant**   (d) **Helephant**

7. A well-known writer:
   (a) **J.K. Rowling**   (b) **J. Bowling**   (c) **L.P. Mowling**   (d) **I.M. Strolling**

8. Which pantomime starts with a cow being sold?
   (a) **Dick Whittington**   (b) **Aladdin**   (c) **Jack and the Beanstalk**
   (d) **Babes in the Wood**

9. Describes an animal that can swim or walk:
   (a) **Amphitheatre**   (b) **Ambidextrous**   (c) **Amphibian**   (d) **Ambulance**

10. Spell the name of a plant scientist:
    (a) **Bottomist**   (b) **Botonist**   (c) **Bottenyst**   (d) **Botanist**

Quiz 15 score

Words and Writing QUIZ

16

Q5

1 Which of these is the infinitive of the verb?
(a) **Baking** (b) **To bake** (c) **Baked** (d) **I was baking**

2 What might you find on a table?
(a) **Cutlass** (b) **Cuttlefish** (c) **Cutlery** (d) **Cudgel**

3 Which is the adjective here?
(a) **Child** (b) **Children** (c) **Childish** (d) **Childishly**

4 Something used to show films:
(a) **Protester** (b) **Preparer** (c) **Producer** (d) **Projector**

5 People standing close together are in a ... what?
(a) **Huddle** (b) **Muddle** (c) **Cuddle** (d) **Puddle**

Q9

6 Which word means 'as clean as can be'?
(a) **Cleaner** (b) **Cleanier** (c) **Cleanish** (d) **Cleanest**

7 Which has the apostrophe in the right place?
(a) **Joes sock's** (b) **Jo'es socks** (c) **Joes socks'** (d) **Joe's socks**

8 What's the opposite of rough?
(a) **Smooth** (b) **Shiny** (c) **Clean** (d) **Smart**

9 What do we call a group of bees?
(a) **Flock** (b) **Swarm** (c) **Herd** (d) **School**

10 The past tense of 'I sing':
(a) **I sung** (b) **I song** (c) **I singed** (d) **I sang**

Q7

Quiz 16 score

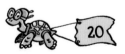

Words and Writing QUIZ

17

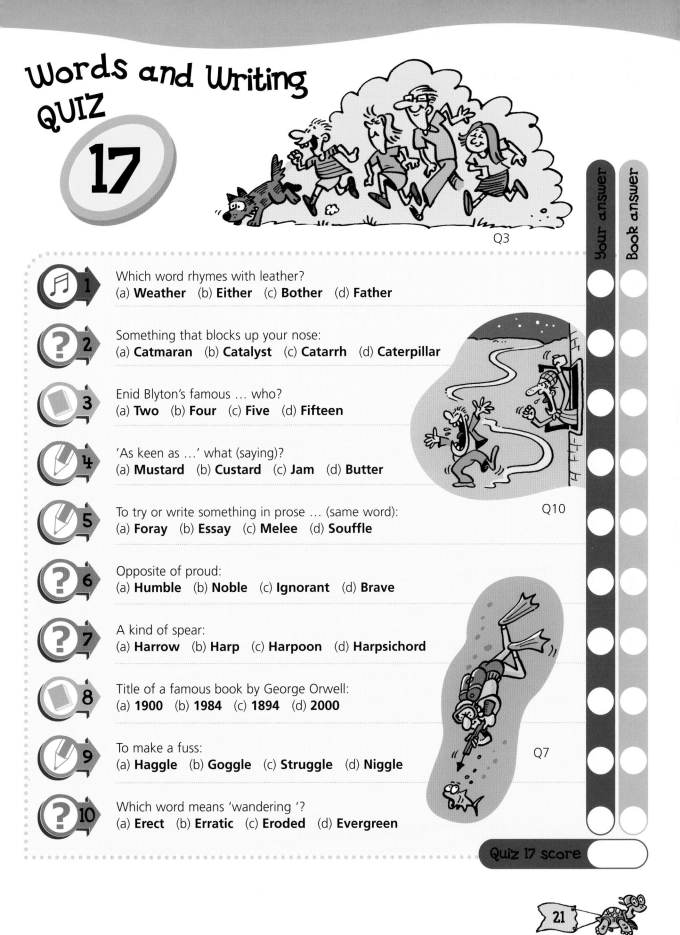

Q3

1 Which word rhymes with leather?
(a) **Weather**   (b) **Either**   (c) **Bother**   (d) **Father**

2 Something that blocks up your nose:
(a) **Catmaran**   (b) **Catalyst**   (c) **Catarrh**   (d) **Caterpillar**

3 Enid Blyton's famous … who?
(a) **Two**   (b) **Four**   (c) **Five**   (d) **Fifteen**

4 'As keen as …' what (saying)?
(a) **Mustard**   (b) **Custard**   (c) **Jam**   (d) **Butter**

5 To try or write something in prose … (same word):
(a) **Foray**   (b) **Essay**   (c) **Melee**   (d) **Souffle**

Q10

6 Opposite of proud:
(a) **Humble**   (b) **Noble**   (c) **Ignorant**   (d) **Brave**

7 A kind of spear:
(a) **Harrow**   (b) **Harp**   (c) **Harpoon**   (d) **Harpsichord**

8 Title of a famous book by George Orwell:
(a) **1900**   (b) **1984**   (c) **1894**   (d) **2000**

9 To make a fuss:
(a) **Haggle**   (b) **Goggle**   (c) **Struggle**   (d) **Niggle**

Q7

10 Which word means 'wandering '?
(a) **Erect**   (b) **Erratic**   (c) **Eroded**   (d) **Evergreen**

Quiz 17 score

Words and Writing QUIZ

18

Q4

 1 A loud noise:
(a) **Din**   (b) **Lilt**   (c) **Tang**   (d) **Aroma**

 2 A writer's pen-name:
(a) **Disguise**   (b) **Nom-de-plume**   (c) **False beard**   (d) **Alibi**

 3 Part two of a film or book:
(a) **Epilogue**   (b) **Introduction**   (c) **Sequel**   (d) **Chapter**

Q7

 4 You hit this in a game of badminton:
(a) **Puck**   (b) **Leather**   (c) **Ball**   (d) **Shuttlecock**

 5 Tool with a curved blade for harvesting grain:
(a) **Sickle**   (b) **Sickie**   (c) **Cycle**   (d) **Cygnet**

 6 Spell 'a cunning plan':
(a) **Strattogerm**   (b) **Stratagem**   (c) **Strattygem**   (d) **Stratterjen**

 7 Spell a young cow:
(a) **Hepher**   (b) **Heifer**   (c) **Wether**   (d) **Heffer**

 8 Slang word meaning to run away:
(a) **Cop**   (b) **Scarper**   (c) **Scoff**   (d) **Kip**

 9 Not likely to study at Hogwarts?
(a) **Meanies**   (b) **Muggles**   (c) **Muppets**   (d) **Misfits**
Q5

 10 Adjective meaning 'from close range':
(a) **Hard and fast**   (b) **Open–ended**   (c) **Point blank**   (d) **Hit and Miss**

Quiz 18 score

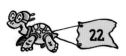

Words and Writing QUIZ

19

Q2

1 A forgetful, disorganized person:
(a) **Brainbox**   (b) **Scatterbrain**   (c) **Chatterbox**   (d) **Fidget**

2 To go on board a ship:
(a) **Embalm**   (b) **Embed**   (c) **Embezzle**   (d) **Embark**

Q5

3 What goes before 'face' to mean 'rub out'?
(a) **ef-**   (b) **in-**   (c) **ex-**   (d) **ab-**

4 Which spelling is correct for a French hat?
(a) **Berry**   (b) **Beret**   (c) **Beri**   (d) **Beray**

5 What would you do with a beverage?
(a) **Drink it**   (b) **Ride it**   (c) **Wear it**   (d) **Read it**

6 Spell the plural of 'vase':
(a) **Vasses**   (b) **Vase's**   (c) **Vasses'**   (d) **Vases**

7 An adjective meaning 'very strange':
(a) **Shocking**   (b) **Weird**   (c) **Various**   (d) **Frequent**

Q9

8 Which of these is not a prefix?
(a) **aero-**   (b) **–archy**   (c) **kilo-**   (d) **ante-**

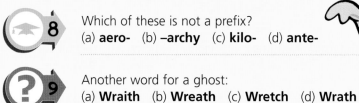

9 Another word for a ghost:
(a) **Wraith**   (b) **Wreath**   (c) **Wretch**   (d) **Wrath**

10 A collection of poems or stories:
(a) **Encyclopedia**   (b) **Epigram**   (c) **Anthology**   (d) **Index**

Quiz 19 score

23

Words and Writing
QUIZ
20

Q9

 1 On a ship, for steering:
(a) **Ruff**   (b) **Ruffle**   (c) **Rudder**   (d) **Rucksack**

 2 Which word rhymes with weasel?
(a) **Woosle**   (b) **Easel**   (c) **Level**   (d) **Weather**

Q2

 3 To make fun of something or someone:
(a) **Copy**   (b) **Admire**   (c) **Compete**   (d) **Mock**

 4 Which of these is usually at the end of a book?
(a) **Prologue**   (b) **Introduction**   (c) **Title**   (d) **Index**

 5 To do with the eye:
(a) **Dental**   (b) **Chronic**   (c) **Optic**   (d) **Mastic**

 6 An ancient Greek shrine:
(a) **Oracle**   (b) **Coracle**   (c) **Monocle**   (d) **Pyramid**

 7 Spell someone who hopes for the best:
(a) **Pessimist**   (b) **Optimist**   (c) **Fortune-teller**   (d) **Pesteemist**

 8 To trick or fool someone:
(a) **To fox**   (b) **To cow**   (c) **To dog**   (d) **To squirrel**

 9 Spell the article of clothing:
(a) **Cloak**   (b) **Cloke**   (c) **Kloak**   (d) **Clook**

 10 Gloomy Dane in a play by Shakespeare:
(a) **Romeo**   (b) **Othello**   (c) **Lear**   (d) **Hamlet**

Q5

Quiz 20 score

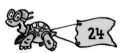

Words and Writing QUIZ

21

Q1

 1 A group of musicians:
(a) **Assembly**   (b) **Ensemble**   (c) **Platoon**   (d) **Squadron**

 2 A lot of fish:
(a) **Shoal**   (b) **Formation**   (c) **Gaggle**   (d) **Herd**

Q2

 3 Describes, or qualifies a noun:
(a) **Pronoun**   (b) **Adverb**   (c) **Adjective**   (d) **Vowel**

 4 Spell the musical instrument:
(a) **Xylophone**   (b) **Zylophone**   (c) **Seilophone**   (d) **Silofone**

 5 A word meaning 'to drive out':
(a) **Explain**   (b) **Explode**   (c) **Expel**   (d) **Expect**

 6 A word lots of us get wrong:
(a) **Nessessary**   (b) **Necessury**   (c) **Neccessery**   (d) **Necessary**

 7 Who wrote *A Christmas Carol*?
(a) **Dahl**   (b) **Dickens**   (c) **Shakespeare**   (d) **Wordsworth**

Q7

 8 Make an adjective from 'empire':
(a) **Imperial**   (b) **Impressive**   (c) **Impish**   (d) **Impudent**

 9 A child whose parents are dead:
(a) **Infant**   (b) **Orphan**   (c) **Evacuee**   (d) **Stepchild**

 10 Which does not mean the same as 'smart'?
(a) **Well-dressed**   (b) **Clever**   (c) **To be sore**   (d) **To cheat**

Quiz 21 score

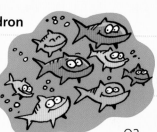

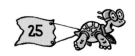

25

Words and Writing QUIZ

22

Your answer

Book answer

 1 Found in a playground:
(a) **Ho-hum**   (b) **See-saw**   (c) **Ha-ha**   (d) **Bye-bye**

 2 The past tense of 'to find':
(a) **Found**   (b) **Funded**   (c) **Finded**   (d) **Fond**

Q3

 3 Old-fashioned word for a chicken, or any bird:
(a) **Fowl**   (b) **Kine**   (c) **Steed**   (d) **Brute**

 4 What's the plural of 'fox'?
(a) **Foxen**   (b) **Foxes**   (c) **Foxs**   (d) **Fox's**

 5 Someone who looks after prisoners:
(a) **Wardrobe**   (b) **Warrior**   (c) **Warden**   (d) **Warlock**

 6 Rhymes with knife:
(a) **Strife**   (b) **Knit**   (c) **Living**   (d) **Cliff**

 7 Where a river starts:
(a) **Sorce**   (b) **Sauce**   (c) **Sortz**   (d) **Source**

 8 Means 'ball-shaped', but can you spell it?
(a) **Ferrical**   (b) **Spherical**   (c) **Sferical**   (d) **Sferrikle**

 9 Scottish writer: Robert Louis …?
(a) **Simpson**   (b) **Stevenson**   (c) **Burns**   (d) **Scott**

Q4

 10 Long poem about Heaven and Hell:
(a) **Journey's End**   (b) **Paradise Lost**   (c) **The Waste Land**
(d) **Canterbury Tales**

 Quiz 22 score

Words and Writing
QUIZ
23

Q1

 1 A black powder:
(a) **Suet**   (b) **Suit**   (c) **Soot**   (d) **Rust**   Q3

 2 Which word sounds like water falling?
(a) **Rustle**   (b) **Bang**   (c) **Rattle**   (d) **Splash**

 3 Which word means 'comfortable'?
(a) **Posy**   (b) **Cosy**   (c) **Rosy**   (d) **Nosey**

 4 Spell the backbone of an animal:
(a) **Spine**   (b) **Spyn**   (c) **Spinney**   (d) **Shin**

 5 A verb meaning to twist threads together: Q9
(a) **Twirl**   (b) **Weave**   (c) **Burrow**   (d) **Unravel**

 6 American word for trousers:
(a) **Vest**   (b) **Kilt**   (c) **Pants**   (d) **Tights**

 7 A kind of poem:
(a) **Elegy**   (b) **Effigy**   (c) **Edifice**   (d) **Education**

 8 Past tense of the verb 'to choose'?
(a) **Choosing**   (b) **Choice**   (c) **Choosed**   (d) **Chose**

 9 How many blind mice were there in the rhyme?
(a) **Three**   (b) **Four and Twenty**   (c) **Two**   (d) **Fifty**

 10 Which word means 'three times'?
(a) **Once**   (b) **Twice**   (c) **Thrice**   (d) **Quadruple**

Quiz 23 score

Words and Writing
QUIZ

 24

Q1

1 Which word has to do with aircraft?
(a) **Aeronautics** (b) **Physics** (c) **Oceanography** (d) **Gymnastics**

2 What's the plural of witch?
(a) **Witchs** (b) **Witchs'** (c) **Witches** (d) **Witch's**

Q10

3 Which spelling is correct?
(a) **Dikshunary** (b) **Dikshonerry** (c) **Dictionary** (d)) **Dickshunari**

4 And what does the answer in question 3 mean?
(a) **Book of maps** (b) **Book of words** (c) **Phone book** (d) **Cookery book**

5 Someone who asks for money in the street:
(a) **Beggar** (b) **Prisoner** (c) **Robber** (d) **Shopper**

6 Who picked a peck of pickled peppers?
(a) **Peter Piper** (b) **Little Boy Blue** (c) **Jack Horner** (d) **Silly Sally**

7 Which word describes a cat?
(a) **Canine** (b) **Feline** (c) **Bovine** (d) **Equine**

8 'The book belonging to Mary': which is correct?
(a) **Marys book** (b) **Mary's book** (c) **Marys' book** (d) **Maryes book**

9 Which of these ends a question?
(a) **?** (b) **"** (c) **!** (d) **(**

Q6

10 Who wrote about Man Friday and Robinson Crusoe?
(a) **Fleming** (b) **Homer** (c) **Defoe** (d) **Cervantes**

Quiz 24 score

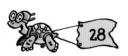 28

Words and Writing QUIZ

25

Q1

| | | Your answer | Book answer |

1 Means 'as dirty as can be':
(a) **Dirtiest** (b) **Dirty** (c) **Dirtier** (d) **Dirtymost**

2 Which has the apostrophe in the wrong place?
(a) **Won't** (b) **Shan't** (c) **Cant'** (d) **Haven't**

Q4

3 Which words always need a capital letter to start?
(a) **Colours** (b) **Science words** (c) **Town names** (d) **Verbs**

4 Their team is better than ... (fill the gap)
(a) **Its** (b) **Their** (c) **Ours** (d) **My**

5 Which of these is an adjective?
(a) **Slowly** (b) **Clever** (c) **Classroom** (d) **Book**

6 What is the opposite of narrow?
(a) **Wide** (b) **Long** (c) **Thin** (d) **Deep**

Q8

7 The future tense of I am:
(a) **I will be** (b) **I were** (c) **I was** (d) **I have been**

8 Which word rhymes with lunch?
(a) **Branch** (b) **Munch** (c) **Launch** (d) **Grunge**

9 As dull as ... what?
(a) **Monday** (b) **Ditchwater** (c) **Cold pizza** (d) **Doomsday**

10 What's a word list in a book called?
(a) **Summary** (b) **Footnote** (c) **Glossary** (d) **Bibliography**

Quiz 25 score

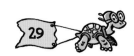

Words and Writing QUIZ

26

Q6

Q5

1 Make an adverb from sad:
(a) **Sadly** (b) **Sadness** (c) **Saddimost** (d) **Saddest**

2 Which word does not mean something to eat?
(a) **Picnic** (b) **Snack** (c) **Sandwich** (d) **Sofa**

3 Which word rhymes with root?
(a) **Flute** (b) **Rot** (c) **Out** (d) **Lout**

4 Which of these is a noun?
(a) **Terrific** (b) **Tree** (c) **Tremble** (d) **Terrible**

5 A word that rhymes with pulley:
(a) **Frilly** (b) **Hilly** (c) **Pretty** (d) **Woolly**

6 Who was Homer the storyteller?
(a) **A Roman** (b) **A Saxon** (c) **A Spaniard** (d) **A Greek**

7 Sound a mouse might make:
(a) **Screech** (b) **Squawk** (c) **Jingle** (d) **Squeak**

8 Find the adjective:
(a) **Posh** (b) **Pet** (c) **Quickly** (d) **Terror**

9 Which of these is a noun?
(a) **Wind** (b) **Windy** (c) **Windiest** (d) **To wind**

Q7

10 Spell the 'saying it right' word
(a) **Pronunseeation** (b) **Prononsesyashun** (c) **Pronunciation**
(d) **Pronounseeaytion**

Quiz 26 score

Words and Writing QUIZ

27

Q4

1 Which of these can be a noun and a verb?
(a) **Cooker**   (b) **Cabbage**   (c) **Saucepan**   (d) **Bowl**

2 Spell the thing you swing in:
(a) **Hummock**   (b) **Himmok**   (c) **Hammock**   (d) **Hemlock**

3 Opposite of proper:
(a) **Improper**   (b) **Abproper**   (c) **Exproper**   (d) **Unproper**

Q7

4 Can be a tool or fly in the air:
(a) **Plane**   (b) **Train**   (c) **Drain**   (d) **Mane**

5 Who had a friend called Big Ears?
(a) **Eeeyore**   (b) **Rupert**   (c) **Joseph**   (d) **Noddy**

6 Word meaning a group of ships and a fast runner?
(a) **Fleet**   (b) **Fast**   (c) **Fling**   (d) **Flotilla**

7 A point of balance:
(a) **Pivot**   (b) **Divot**   (c) **Border**   (d) **Summit**

Q2

8 'Trousers of the boys' – which of these is correct?
(a) **Boys trousers**   (b) **Boys' trousers**   (c) **Boy's trousers**   (d) **Boys trousers'**

9 What's the plural of disco?
(a) **Disco**   (b) **Disco's**   (c) **Discoes**   (d) **Discos**

10 A large jug:
(a) **Basin**   (b) **Decanter**   (c) **Pitcher**   (d) **Tumbler**

Quiz 27 score

Words and Writing
QUIZ
28

Q2

1 A form of verse:
(a) **Couple**   (b) **Souffle**   (c) **Couplet**   (d) **Gavotte**

Q3

2 An adjective meaning 'quick and clever':
(a) **Sleek**   (b) **Fast**   (c) **Brutal**   (d) **Brainy**

3 Spell the word correctly (to mean 'writing materials')
(a) **Stashunery**   (b) **Stationery**   (c) **Stationary**   (d) **Stationairy**

4 Which can be a noun and a verb?
(a) **Span**   (b) **Spade**   (c) **Spa**   (d) **Spaghetti**

5 Which is the odd one out (not a writer)?
(a) **David Hockney** (b) **Michael Morpurgo** (c) **Shirley Hughes** (d) **Ted Hughes**

6 Which word means 'red coloured'?
(a) **Aquamarine**   (b) **Ruddy**   (c) **Azure**   (d) **Ashen**

7 Which of these is not a comparative?
(a) **Bigger**   (b) **Louder**   (c) **Lovely**   (d) **Brighter**

8 Spell the stuff you rub on aching muscles:
(a) **Linoleum**   (b) **Lingerie**   (c) **Linameant**   (d) **Liniment**

Q8

9 A prefix meaning 'backward':
(a) **Ergo-**   (b) **Intro-**   (c) **Extra-**   (d) **Retro-**

10 Who or what does a misanthropist hate?
(a) **Everybody**   (b) **Animals**   (c) **Ants**   (d) **Fog**

Quiz 28 score

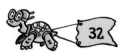

32

Chart Your Scores

	1	2	3	4	5	6	7	8	9	10
Quiz 1										
Quiz 2										
Quiz 3										
Quiz 4										
Quiz 5										
Quiz 6										
Quiz 7										
Quiz 8										
Quiz 9										
Quiz 10										
Quiz 11										
Quiz 12										
Quiz 13										
Quiz 14										
Quiz 15										
Quiz 16										
Quiz 17										
Quiz 18										
Quiz 19										
Quiz 20										
Quiz 21										
Quiz 22										
Quiz 23										
Quiz 24										
Quiz 25										
Quiz 26										
Quiz 27										
Quiz 28										

Homework Champions

Using Numbers

Key to subject icons

 Adding and subtracting

 Measuring

 Multiplying and dividing

 Puzzles and problems

 Fractions and decimals

 Amazing numbers

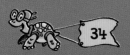

Using Numbers
QUIZ
1

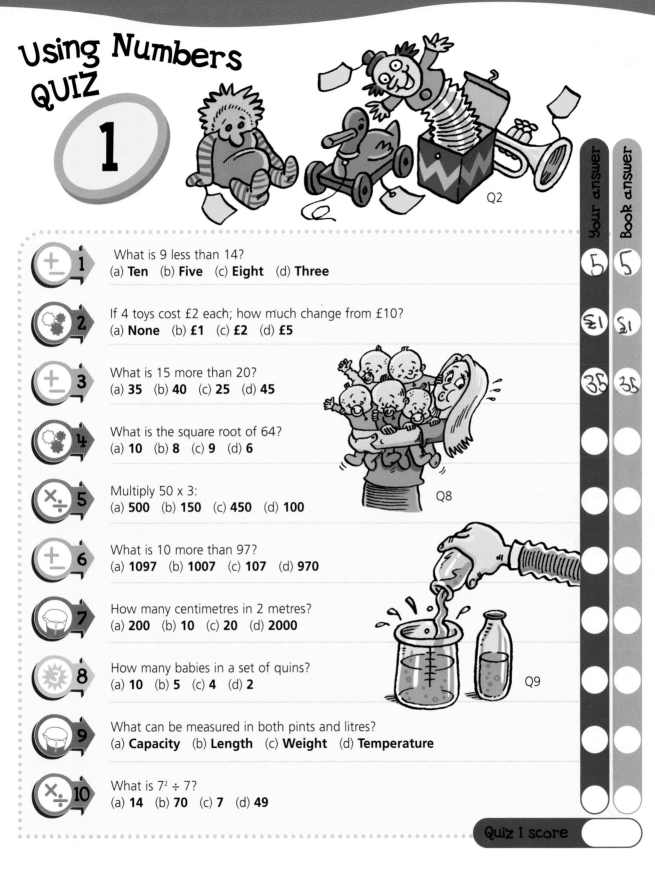

Q2

	Your answer	Book answer

1 What is 9 less than 14?
(a) **Ten** (b) **Five** (c) **Eight** (d) **Three**
Your answer: 5 *Book answer:* 5

2 If 4 toys cost £2 each; how much change from £10?
(a) **None** (b) **£1** (c) **£2** (d) **£5**
Your answer: £2 *Book answer:* £2

3 What is 15 more than 20?
(a) **35** (b) **40** (c) **25** (d) **45**
Your answer: 35 *Book answer:* 35

Q8

4 What is the square root of 64?
(a) **10** (b) **8** (c) **9** (d) **6**

5 Multiply 50 x 3:
(a) **500** (b) **150** (c) **450** (d) **100**

6 What is 10 more than 97?
(a) **1097** (b) **1007** (c) **107** (d) **970**

7 How many centimetres in 2 metres?
(a) **200** (b) **10** (c) **20** (d) **2000**

8 How many babies in a set of quins?
(a) **10** (b) **5** (c) **4** (d) **2**

Q9

9 What can be measured in both pints and litres?
(a) **Capacity** (b) **Length** (c) **Weight** (d) **Temperature**

10 What is $7^2 \div 7$?
(a) **14** (b) **70** (c) **7** (d) **49**

Quiz 1 score

Using Numbers
QUIZ

2

Q1

 1 What does km stand for?
(a) **Kilometre** (b) **Kilowatt** (c) **Kilomile** (d) **Kilominute**

 2 How would a Roman have written 10?
(a) **V** (b) **X** (c) **I** (d) **10**

 3 What is ¾ as a decimal?
(a) **0.30** (b) **0.44** (c) **0.75** (d) **0.95**

Q2

 4 What has 360 degrees?
(a) **A circle** (b) **A triangle** (c) **A thermometer** (d) **A straight line**

 5 How many digits in '2004'?
(a) **2** (b) **4** (c) **0** (d) **1**

 6 How many days are there in 3 weeks?
(a) **14** (b) **7** (c) **28** (d) **21**

 7 What is 9 less than 21?
(a) **30** (b) **12** (c) **15** (d) **13**

 8 How many players in a tennis doubles match?
(a) **6** (b) **2** (c) **8** (d) **4**

Q8

 9 How many more is 39 than 15?
(a) **24** (b) **15** (c) **29** (d) **30**

 10 What is (15 x 5) added to (100 x 3) ?
(a) **550** (b) **325** (c) **320** (d) **375**

Quiz 2 score

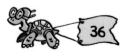

Using Numbers
QUIZ
3

Q3

1 How many sides has a triangle?
(a) **1**   (b) **2**   (c) **3**   (d) **4**

2 70 − 40 = ?
(a) **20**   (b) **30**   (c) **40**   (d) **50**

Q1

3 Two dogs; how many legs?
(a) **6**   (b) **10**   (c) **14**   (d) **8**

4 Multiply 13 by 3:
(a) **33**   (b) **39**   (c) **36**   (d) **35**

5 Add 15 and 15:
(a) **35**   (b) **20**   (c) **30**   (d) **150**

6 What is 10 x 3.75?
(a) **37l**   (b) **37.5**   (c) **375**   (d) **3750**

7 55 + 15 + 173 = ?
(a) **551**   (b) **608**   (c) **253**   (d) **243**

Q8

8 What's the next number: 7, 14, 28, 56, …?
(a) **63**   (b) **72**   (c) **112**   (d) **144**

9 What is 25 x 10?
(a) **250**   (b) **251**   (c) **2510**   (d) **35**

10 If a jar holds 50 sweets and 6 children each eat 5 sweets, how many are left?
(a) **5**   (b) **10**   (c) **15**   (d) **20**

Quiz 3 score

Using Numbers QUIZ

Q1

 1 Add 4 + 6 + 10:
(a) **460**   (b) **100**   (c) **56**   (d) **20**

 2 How many halves in 4?
(a) **8**   (b) **2**   (c) **6**   (d) **10**

 3 Multiply ³⁄₄ by 2:
(a) **1¼**   (b) **1½**   (c) **1**   (d) **2³⁄₄**

 4 Which of these isn't a prime number?
(a) **5**   (b) **2**   (c) **17**   (d) **20**

Q2

 5 (9 x 9) + 7 = ?
(a) **88**   (b) **52**   (c) **79**   (d) **135**

 6 Add 4 + 4 + 4 + 4:
(a) **44**   (b) **16**   (c) **12**   (d) **24**

 7 What is 2 to the power of 2?
(a) **8**   (b) **22**   (c) **6**   (d) **4**

Q8

 8 What does adding 15 to 35 give you?
(a) **46**   (b) **50**   (c) **60**   (d) **71**

 9 Which unit is the closest to a metre in length?
(a) **Mile**   (b) **Foot**   (c) **Yard**   (d) **Inch**

 10 Which is the same as (100 − 55) x 2?
(a) **9 x 10**   (b) **(100 + 10) x 2**   (c) **150 − 65**   (d) **(50 + 50) x 1**

Your answer

Book answer

Quiz 4 score

Using Numbers QUIZ

5

Q3

	Your answer	Book answer

1 How do you find the area of a rectangle?
(a) **Length x 3**   (b) **Width x 2**   (c) **Length x Width**   (d) **Halve one side**

2 How many sides has an octagon?
(a) **4**   (b) **6**   (c) **8**   (d) **10**

3 What do we call picture-maths?
(a) **Grafts**   (b) **Graphs**   (c) **Grapes**   (d) **Gripes**

4 What is ⅛ of 96?
(a) **48**   (b) **9**   (c) **12**   (d) **16**   Q7

5 What units do we use to measure angles?
(a) **Points**   (b) **Centimetres**   (c) **Kilos**   (d) **Degrees**

6 Which of these is a complete turn?
(a) **A revolution**   (b) **A reflex**   (c) **A right angle**   (d) **A tangent**

7 Which scientist is famous for his rule about angles?
(a) **Pythagoras**   (b) **Darwin**   (c) **Newton**   (d) **Einstein**

8 Which of these has to do with maths?
(a) **Theory of evolution**   (b) **Symmetry**   (c) **Queensberry Rules**
(d) **Custer's Last Stand**

Q8

9 What is 9.1 + 3.4?
(a) **13.00**   (b) **91.34**   (c) **9,134**   (d) **12.5**

10 What do we call a parallelogram with two adjacent sides equal?
(a) **Rhombus**   (b) **Rebus**   (c) **Rhinoceros**   (d) **Right angle**

Quiz 5 score

Using Numbers
QUIZ

2 4 6 8 ...

Q1

1
Complete the sequence: 2, 4, 6, 8, ...
(a) **10**   (b) **12**   (c) **9**   (b) **7**

2
How many halves in 6 wholes?
(a) **6**   (b) **9**   (c) **12**   (d) **15**

Q9

3
If x + 20 = 42, what is x?
(a) **2**   (b) **22**   (c) **30**   (d) **18**

4
What is 3 million x 2 million?
(a) **6 million**   (b) **5 million**   (c) **5 thousand**   (d) **320 thousand**

5
7 + 2 is the same as which of these sums?
(a) **12 – 3**   (b) **5 + 5**   (c) **6 + 2**   (d) **7 – 4**

6
What is the same as 3 x 4?
(a) **3 x 3**   (b) **5 x 2**   (c) **6 x 2**   (d) **7 x 2**

7
How much less than 25 is 19?
(a) **6**   (b) **9**   (c) **20**   (d) **5**

8
What is 150 ÷ 50?
(a) **200**   (b) **3**   (c) **100**   (d) **4**

Q3

9
How many inches made a foot?
(a) **10**   (b) **24**   (c) **12**   (d) **18**

10
Which of these was a mathematician of the 1800s?
(a) **George Boole**   (b) **George Michael**   (c) **George Best**   (d) **George Bush**

Quiz 6 score

40

Using Numbers QUIZ

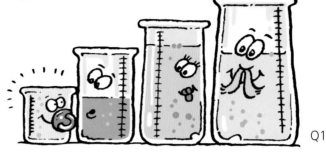

Q1

 1 Which is the smallest ?
(a) **2.5 ml**   (b) **5 ml**   (c) **10 ml**   (d) **15 ml**

 2 How many centilitres in a litre?
(a) **10**   (b) **100**   (c) **1,000**   (d) **20**

 3 Which of these has the most zeros?
(a) **1 million**   (b) **1 thousand**   (c) **10 thousand**   (d) **10 million**

 4 What is half of 24?
(a) **10**   (b) **18**   (c) **12**   (d) **16**

Q4

 5 How many digits in the answer to 3 x 20 x 10?
(a) **3**   (b) **2**   (c) **4**   (d) **6**

 6 10 x ? = 1000
(a) **10**   (b) **100**   (c) **200**   (d) **500**

 7 Add 3 to 10, then double the answer:
(a) **26**   (b) **13**   (c) **30**   (d) **18**

 8 Take 7 away from 49:
(a) **39**   (b) **40**   (c) **46**   (d) **42**

 9 What is 7 x 6?
(a) **36**   (b) **40**   (c) **49**   (d) **42**

Q7

 10 What is the next prime number after: 3, 5, 7, …?
(a) **9**   (b) **17**   (c) **8**   (d) **11**

Quiz 7 score

41

Using Numbers
QUIZ

8

Q5

 1   What is 144 ÷ 12?
(a) **12**   (b) **10**   (c) **14**   (d) **20**

20 cm

 2   Which does not belong in this set?
(a) **3 x 3**   (b) **18 ÷ 2**   (c) **4 + 5**   (d) **21 – 10**

 3   What number is 13 more than 90?
(a) **83**   (b) **103**   (c) **12 3**   (d) **113**

Q10

10 cm

 4   Multiply 12 by 5:
(a) **125**   (b) **70**   (c) **60**   (d) **17**

 5   If a farmer sells 109 of 140 sheep, how many are left?
(a) **31**   (b) **24**   (c) **25**   (d) **15**

 6   What is 104 more than 155?
(a) **219**   (b) **172**   (c) **259**   (d) **248**

FEBRUARY

7   40 + ? = 160
(a) **20**   (b) **150**   (c) **130**   (d) **120**

 8   Which of these is the smallest?
(a) **1 cm**   (b) **1 km**   (c) **1 m**   (d) **10 cm**

Q9

 9   How many days in two weeks?
(a) **7**   (b) **10**   (c) **14**   (d) **21**

10   What is the area of a book 20 x 10 cm?
(a) **250 cm^2**   (b) **200 cm^2**   (c) **100 cm^2**   (d) **1000 cm^2**

Quiz 8 score

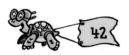

Using Numbers QUIZ

9

Your answer | **Book answer**

 1 Count 4 back from 17 and you have …?
(a) **13**　(b) **21**　(c) **12**　(d) **9**

 2 Which symbol means 'divide'?
(a) **+**　(b) **x**　(c) **÷**　(d) **?**

 3 Which month never has more than 29 days?
(a) **January**　(b) **February**　(c) **December**　(d) **September**

Q7

 4 Counting in 3s, what comes after 15?
(a) **16**　(b) **18**　(c) **17**　(d) **21**

 5 What is 50% of 50 cakes?
(a) **5**　(b) **10**　(c) **25**　(d) **45**

 6 Add 10 to 799:
(a) **789**　(b) **815**　(c) **809**　(d) **7990**

 7 How many 4s are there in 48?
(a) **10**　(b) **12**　(c) **13**　(d) **14**

 8 What is 37 less than 77?
(a) **20**　(b) **40**　(c) **49**　(d) **55**

Q5

 9 What number comes next; 48, 24, 12, 6, …?
(a) **0**　(b) **2**　(c) **4**　(d) **3**

 10 What is the square root of 25?
(a) **5**　(b) **20**　(c) **10**　(d) **2**

Quiz 9 score

Using Numbers QUIZ

10

Q1

1 How many £2 coins make £10?
(a) **3**   (b) **5**   (c) **4**   (d) **10**

2 What is 2 + 4 ÷ 3?
(a) **9**   (b) **2**   (c) **18**   (d) **5**

3 How many days in 2 years (no leap years) ?
(a) **365**   (b) **1000**   (c) **730**   (d) **800**

4 Which is the 4th month of the year?
(a) **March**   (b) **January**   (c) **July**   (d) **April**

Q4

5 How many more is 35 than 28?
(a) **7**   (b) **5**   (c) **10**   (d) **19**

6 What is half of 100 rabbits?
(a) **10**   (b) **25**   (c) **40**   (d) **50**

7 Fill in the next number: 3, 6, 12, …?
(a) **15**   (b) **20**   (c) **24**   (d) **48**

Q10

£1.75

8 Which number pair has a difference of 6?
(a) **3:9**   (b) **2:7**   (c) **14:9**   (d) **3:8**

9 What is 444,799 to the nearest thousand?
(a) **444,000**   (b) **500,000**   (c) **445,000**   (d) **400,000**

10 Which coin set = £1.75?
(a) **£1 + £1 +50p**   (b) **£2 + 10p**   (c) **£1 + 50p + 20p + 5p**   (d) **£1 + 20p + 5p**

Quiz 10 score

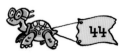

Using Numbers QUIZ

11

Q5

 1 What is 15 ÷ 3?
(a) **45**   (b) **12**   (c) **5**   (d) **1**

 2 How many 25s are there in 200?
(a) **8**   (b) **9**   (c) **10**   (d) **11**

 3 Which is biggest?
(a) **6 x 3**   (b) **7 x 4**   (c) **8 x 2**   (d) **9 x 3**

 4 How much greater is 150 than 70?
(a) **70**   (b) **80**   (c) **90**   (d) **100**

 5 How much change from £10 from six £1.00 ice creams?
(a) **£2**   (b) **£4**   (c) **£6**   (d) **£1**

Q7

 6 Which is the smallest?
(a) **6 x 50**   (b) **7 x 50**   (c) **3 x 110**   (d) **4 x 30**

 7 How many horns have 12 billy goats?
(a) **12**   (b) **36**   (c) **24**   (d) **48**

 8 What does 'kilo' stand for (as in kilometre)?
(a) **10**   (b) **100**   (c) **1,000**   (d) **1,000,000**

 9 How many hot dogs would make three dozen?
(a) **24**   (b) **36**   (c) **44**   (d) **30**

Q10

10 Divide 12,560 sheep into groups of 40; how many groups?
(a) **356**   (b) **314**   (c) **34.6**   (d) **3140**

Quiz 11 score

45

Using Numbers QUIZ

12

Q10

		Your answer	Book answer

 1 What's half of 44?
(a) **20** (b) **22** (c) **24** (d) **26**

 2 In which century was the year 1066?
(a) **9th** (b) **10th** (c) **11th** (d) **12th**

 3 How many runs in a cricket century?
(a) **10** (b) **50** (c) **150** (d) **100**

 4 Which decimal measure is less than 1½?
(a) **1.56** (b) **1.25** (c) **1.75** (d) **1.68**

 5 How many quarter-slices in nine pizzas?
(a) **36** (b) **30** (c) **27** (d) **45**

Q5

 6 How much is half of £4.00?
(a) **£2.00** (b) **£1.00** (c) **£8.00** (d) **£3.00**

 7 Take 140 away from 280:
(a) **140** (b) **120** (c) **100** (d) **80**

 8 What are seven nines?
(a) **36** (b) **70** (c) **81** (d) **63**

 9 How many legs do six cats have between them?
(a) **12** (b) **24** (c) **10** (d) **16**

 10 What are the two arms of a line graph called?
(a) **Axles** (b) **Axes** (c) **Corners** (d) **Angles**

Quiz 12 score

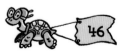

Using Numbers
QUIZ

13

Q4

 1 Add 10 to 97:
(a) **177**   (b) **87**   (c) **107**   (d) **157**

 2 What is 3 x 150?
(a) **650**   (b) **450**   (c) **500**   (d) **250**

 3 Multiply 10 x 10 x 3:
(a) **300**   (b) **23**   (c) **3,000**   (d) **130**

Q1

 4 What date came 2 years after January 1999?
(a) **January 2000**   (b) **January 1998**   (c) **January 2001**   (d) **January 2003**

 5 How do you write thirteen million five hundred thousand in numbers?
(a) **13,500,000**   (b) **13m 500k**   (c) **13.5**   (d) **1,350,000**

 6 What's the difference between 7 and 12?
(a) **3**   (b) **5**   (c) **19**   (d) **2**

 7 Round 9,789 to the nearest 10:
(a) **9,700**   (b) **9,800**   (c) **10,000**   (d) **9,000**

 8 What is 0.25 as a fraction?
(a) $\frac{1}{2}$ (b) $\frac{1}{4}$ (c) $\frac{1}{3}$ (d) $\frac{2}{3}$

Q3

 9 What number is half of sixty?
(a) **30**   (b) **20**   (c) **120**   (d) **16**

 10 Divide 13,680 by 570
(a) **55**   (b) **30**   (c) **27**   (d) **24**

Quiz 13 score

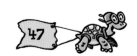

Using Numbers QUIZ 14

 1 Two quarters make one …: what?
(a) **Whole** (b) **Half** (c) **Third** (d) **Sixth**

 2 What is 25% of 200?
(a) **100** (b) **60** (c) **50** (d) **25**

$$14.5 \times 2$$

Q3

 3 Double 14.5:
(a) **29** (b) **22** (c) **30** (d) **28**

 4 What time p.m. is 15.45?
(a) **Quarter past three** (b) **Three o' clock** (c) **Half past three**
(d) **Quarter to four**

 5 Subtract 13 from 27:
(a) **14** (b) **12** (c) **9** (d) **21**

 6 Halve 144:
(a) **100** (b) **72** (c) **68** (d) **14.4**

 7 What is 9^2?
(a) **76** (b) **64** (c) **112** (d) **81**

 8 How many eggs in two dozen?
(a) **36** (b) **20** (c) **12** (d) **24**

Q8

 9 What is 110 more than 972?
(a) **982** (b) **1082** (c) **1972** (d) **1022**

 10 Which of these is not a type of diagram used in maths?
(a) **Jane** (b) **Venn** (c) **Carroll** (d) **Tree**

Quiz 14 score

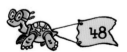

Using Numbers
QUIZ

15

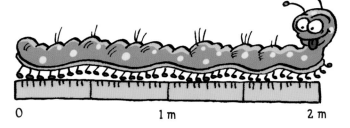

0   1 m   2 m

Q2

1 What is 15 less than 45?
(a) **40** (b) **20** (c) **10** (d) **30**

10,000,000"

2 How many centimetres in 2 metres?
(a) **20** (b) **200** (c) **2000** (d) **2,000,000**

3 What is the remainder when you divide 151 by 5?
(a) **51** (b) **1** (c) **11** (d) **0**

4 Divide 156 by 4:
(a) **30** (b) **47** (c) **39** (d) **58**

Q10

5 Add 157 and 294:
(a) **451** (b) **329** (c) **573** (d) **477**

6 What is 5^2 x 10?
(a) **150** (b) **250** (c) **300** (d) **350**

7 What is one-tenth as a percentage?
(a) **5%** (b) **100**% (c) **1%** (d) **10%**

8 What is double 353?
(a) **696** (b) **706** (c) **709** (d) **699**

Q6

9 What is 2 x 5 x 10?
(a) **250** (b) **100** (c) **700** (d) **50**

10 How many zeros when you write ten million in numbers?
(a) **2** (b) **4** (c) **7** (d) **10**

Quiz 15 score

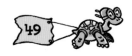

49

Using Numbers
QUIZ

16

Q7

 1 Convert 1.47 m to centimetres:
(a) **14.7** cm (b) **147 cm** (c) **14,700 cm** (d) **0.147 cm**

 2 Subtract 47 from 92:
(a) **29** (b) **35** (c) **45** (d) **42**

 3 Double 250 is …?
(a) **500** (b) **125** (c) **750** (d) **2500**

 4 How many degrees in a right angle?
(a) **45°** (b) **70°** (c) **180°** (d) **90°**

Q9

 5 What is ½ as a decimal?
(a) **0.25** (b) **0.5** (c) **0.1** (d) **0.2**

 6 Which is the smallest set?
(a) **3 + 3 + 3** (b) **4 + 4** (c) **2 + 2+ 2** (d) **3 + 3 + 4**

 7 How many legs on 4 camels?
(a) **9** (b) **8** (c) **16** (d) **14**

 8 How long are 7 decades, in years?
(a) **30** (b) **70** (c) **140** (d) **21**

Q3

 9 How many players in 2 soccer teams (without subs)?
(a) **22** (b) **24** (c) **11** (d) **30**

 10 If x -14 = 39, what's x?
(a) **25** (b) **62** (c) **49** (d) **53**

Quiz 16 score

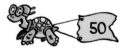

Using Numbers
QUIZ
17

Q2

 1 Subtract 26 from 75:
(a) **49**   (b) **32**   (c) **56**   (d) **101**

 2 How many tails do 11 whales have?
(a) **22**   (b) **11**   (c) **33**   (d) **44**

 3 How many 100s in 5000?
(a) **5**   (b) **500**   (c) **15**   (d) **50**

Q7

 4 Multiply 600 x 600:
(a) **360,000**   (b) **3600**   (c) **360,000,000**   (d) **3.6 billion**

 5 How many thirds in two wholes?
(a) **3**   (b) **9**   (c) **6**   (d) **12**

 6 What's next on this number line: 144, 72, 36, 18, ...?
(a) **10**   (b) **0**   (c) **9**   (d) **6**

 7 How many 10s are there in 56?
(a) **6**   (b) **5**   (c) **4**   (d) **3**

 8 What comes next: 3, 7, 11, 15, ...?
(a) **16**   (b) **30**   (c) **10**   (d) **19**

 9 How many odd numbers come before 14?
(a) **0**   (b) **2**   (c) **4**   (d) **7**

Q8

10 What's the biggest number you can make from 3, 2, 8?
(a) **832**   (b) **328**   (c) **283**   (d) **823**

Quiz 17 score

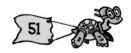

51

Using Numbers
QUIZ
18

$(4+2+11)-7=$

Q2

 1 What is 200 x 6?
(a) **2006**   (b) **1200**   (c) **206**   (d) **24,000**

 2 Solve the sum: $(4 + 2 + 11) - 7 = ?$
(a) **5**   (b) **15**   (c) **10**   (d) **24**

 3 Add 9 + 2 + 10 + 6:
(a) **25**   (b) **21**   (c) **13**   (d) **27**

Q8

 4 What is 3 x 33?
(a) **66**   (b) **99**   (c) **33**   (d) **300**

 5 What is 7 x 7 x 7?
(a) **144**   (b) **213**   (c) **343**   (d) **648**

 6 Divide 36 by 5 and what's left over?
(a) **4**   (b) **2**   (c) **0**   (d) **1**

 7 How many days in 3 weeks?
(a) **21**   (b) **20**   (c) **18**   (d) **14**

 8 What's the fewest dots you must join to make a triangle?
(a) **2**   (b) **3**   (c) **4**   (d) **5**

Q9

 9 What time is 4 hours before 8 a.m.?
(a) **12 a.m.**   (b) **4 a.m.**   (c) **4 p.m.**   (d) **2 a.m.**

 10 5 x 4a= 200: what's the value of a?
(a) **0**   (b) **20**   (c) **10**   (d) **5**

Quiz 18 score

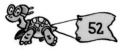

Using Numbers
QUIZ
19

Your answer | **Book answer**

 1 How many fives in 35?
(a) **4**   (b) **5**   (c) **6**   (d) **7**

 2 How many degrees in half a circle (semi-circle) ?
(a) **360**   (b) **180**   (c) **90**   (d) **45**

Q2

 3 10 children eat 50 buns; what's the average 'eat'?
(a) **500**   (b) **5**   (c) **50**   (d) **10**

 4 What's the nearest estimate to an average man's height?
(a) **1.8 m**   (b) **1.8 cm**   (c) **1.8 cm**   (d) **18 m**

 5 What is half of 72?
(a) **144**   (b) **24**   (c) **36**   (d) **60**

 6 What is 41 x 17?
(a) **697**   (b) **589**   (c) **362**   (d) **499**

 7 Can you work out what comes next: 18, 24, 30, 36, …?
(a) **40**   (b) **42**   (c) **44**   (d) **48**

 8 Which is the smallest fraction?
(a) $^1/_4$ (b) $^1/_2$ (c) $^3/_{16}$ (d) $^3/_{10}$

9 If x = 12 and y = 35, what is (2x + y) – 19?   Q3
(a) **17**   (b) **40**   (c) **2**   (d) **10**

 10 Which set is the largest ?
(a) **20 + 12 + 5**   (b) **10 + 10 + 10**   (c) **13 + 13 + 3**   (d) **11 + 13 + 14**

Quiz 19 score

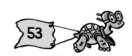

53

Using Numbers QUIZ

20

Q8

1 How long does a trip of 1500 km take at average speed of 50 km per hour?
(a) **5 hours**   (b) **11 hours**   (c) **10 hours**   (d) **30 hours**

2 Which is the next number: 100, 150, 250, 400, …
(a) **350**   (b) **450**   (c) **800**   (d) **600**

Q6

3 What year will come immediately before 2100?
(a) **1999**   (b) **2099**   (c) **2000**   (d) **2101**

4 What is 177 – 159?
(a) **15**   (b) **16**   (c) **18**   (d) **20**

5 Which is biggest?
(a) **1000 x 5**   (b) **50 x 100**   (c) **10 x 5000**   (d) **100 x 10**

6 Four ice creams cost £4.80; how much is one?
(a) **£2.00**   (b) **£1.20**   (c) **£2.40**   (d) **£1.35**

7 How many 16s are there in 960?
(a) **10**   (b) **30**   (c) **40**   (d) **60**

8 If each jar holds 45 sweets, what is the total number of sweets in 3 jars?
(a) **115**   (b) **125**   (c) **135**   (d) **145**

9 What's 90 plus 150 divided by 6?
(a) **300**   (b) **75**   (c) **60**   (d) **40**

10 What is half of $4\frac{1}{2}$ hours?
(a) **$1\frac{1}{2}$**   (b) **$2\frac{1}{4}$**   (c) **$2\frac{1}{2}$**   (d) **$2\frac{3}{4}$**

Quiz 20 score

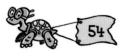

Using Numbers
QUIZ

21

Q1

1 How many ears are there on 17 rabbits?
(a) **17** (b) **44** (c) **34** (d) **68**

2 What is 10.30 pm on the 24-hour clock?
(a) **10.30** (b) **14.00** (c) **20.30** (d) **22.30**

Q2

3 Which is biggest?
(a) **0.78** (b) **0.078** (c) **7.8** (d) **78**

4 Divide 99 by 10; how much is left over?
(a) **0** (b) **1** (c) **5** (d) **9**

5 What did C stand for in Roman numerals?
(a) **50** (b) **10** (c) **1000** (d) **100**

6 How many disciples did Jesus have, according to the Bible?
(a) **6** (b) **7** (c) **12** (d) **100**

7 What's one-third of 189?
(a) **72** (b) **63** (c) **49** (d) **53**

Q9

8 What must you add to 750 to make 1000?
(a) **100** (b) **250** (c) **125** (d) **500**

9 Which number is said to be 'unlucky'?
(a) **7** (b) **13** (c) **10** (d) **101**

10 If there are 12 pencils in a box, how many in 14 boxes?
(a) **168** (b) **200** (c) **140** (d) **156**

Quiz 21 score

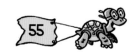

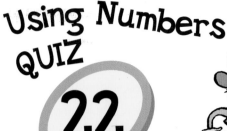

Using Numbers
QUIZ
22

Q1

 1 The Magnificent …? (film title)
(a) **6** (b) **100** (c) **7** (d) **1,000,000**

 2 How much less than 1400 is 950?
(a) **450** (b) **550** (c) **650** (d) **200**

Q4

 3 If a 150 litre tank is half empty, how much is left?
(a) **100 litres** (b) **50 litres** (c) **75 litres** (d) **80 litres**

 4 How many kings of England have been called Henry?
(a) **4** (b) **5** (c) **3** (d) **8**

 5 What is one-third of 333?
(a) **33** (b) **66** (c) **111** (d) **123**

 6 What must you add to 7500 to make 12,500?
(a) **500** (b) **5000** (c) **7000** (d) **7500**

 7 If $x + 129 = 200$, how much is x?
(a) **52** (b) **67** (c) **71** (d) **78**

 8 A stitch in time saves … how many (saying)?
(a) **4** (b) **6** (c) **9** (d) **14**

 9 How many 60s are there in 360?
(a) **8** (b) **4** (c) **6** (d) **9**

Q8

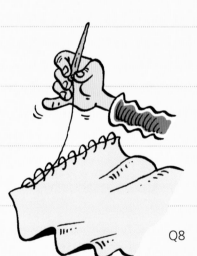

 10 In Olympic rowing, what's the most rowers in one racing boat?
(a) **4** (b) **6** (c) **8** (d) **10**

Quiz 22 score

Using Numbers QUIZ

23

1 Add 5 to −5 and what's the answer?
(a) **0**   (b) **−10**   (c) **1**   (d) **10**

2 Write 463 to the nearest 50:
(a) **500**   (b) **400**   (c) **450**   (d) **550**

Q7

3 How much do two T-shirts cost, at £5.75 each?
(a) **£3.00**   (b) **£2.50**   (c) **£10.00**   (d) **£11.50**

4 How many tens are there in 1750?
(a) **17.5**   (b) **175**   (c) **1750**   (d) **17**

5 172 − 168 =?
(a) **12**   (b) **4**   (c) **14**   (d) **8**

Q8

6 What is 70% of 200?
(a) **150**   (b) **200**   (c) **140**   (d) **400**

7 How many 20p coins make £3.40?
(a) **30**   (b) **13**   (c) **17**   (d) **15**

8 What might you measure in hectares?
(a) **Your feet**   (b) **A field**   (c) **A bag of shopping**   (d) **Elephants**

9 If a=5 and b=20, what is a x b?
(a) **15**   (b) **25**   (c) **100**   (d) **205**

10 Which of these is true of a 'plane figure'?
(a) **Always round**   (b) **Flies**   (c) **Flat surface**   (d) **Equal sides**

Quiz 23 score

Q3

Using Numbers
QUIZ
24

Q2

 1 What's (15 x 4) x 9?
(a) **540**   (b) **171**   (c) **99**   (d) **600**

Q6

 2 Five horses; how many ears?
(a) **5**   (b) **8**   (c) **10**   (d) **12**

 3 Which is smallest?
(a) **17 – 9**   (b) **19 – 12**   (c) **21 – 14**   (d) **23 – 17**

 4 Which is the most famous date in US history?
(a) **1066**   (b) **1588**   (c) **1776**   (d) **1900**

 5 Add 17 and 15, then double the answer
(a) **48**   (b) **64**   (c) **76**   (d) **108**

Q8

 6 How many legs are there on 7 beetles?
(a) **14**   (b) **49**   (c) **42**   (d) **56**

 7 What number comes next: 15,000; 1500; 150; 15, …?
(a) **0**   (b) **10**   (c) **1.5**   (d) **5**

 8 How many leaves has a 'lucky' clover?
(a) **1**   (b) **4**   (c) **8**   (d) **13**

 9 What's the area of a garden 15 m x 25 m?
(a) **500 sq m**   (b) **350 sq m**   (c) **275 sq km**   (d) **375 sq m**

 10 How many vertices are there on a cube?
(a) **2**   (b) **4**   (c) **6**   (d) **8**

Quiz 24 score

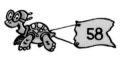

Using Numbers QUIZ

25

Your answer   **Book answer**

 1 A chicken lays an egg a day for 8 weeks; how many eggs?
(a) **40**   (b) **42**   (c) **48**   (d) **56**

 2 What's half of 1272?
(a) **536**   (b) **636**   (c) **586**   (d) **648**

Q7

 3 Multiply 14 x 6
(a) **80**   (b) **82**   (c) **84**   (d) **86**

 4 Add 14 + 15 + 16 + 17
(a) **52**   (b) **62**   (c) **72**   (d) **82**

 5 What's the lowest throw with three dice?
(a) **5**   (b) **4**   (c) **3**   (d) **2**

 6 How many kilograms in one tonne?
(a) **10**   (b) **100**   (c) **1000**   (d) **10,000**

Q9

 7 Add 6 + 15, then double your answer
(a) **40**   (b) **25**   (c) **52**   (d) **42**

 8 Which was not a leap year?
(a) **2004**   (b) **1996**   (c) **1998**   (d) **1992**

 9 How many right angles are there in 4 squares?
(a) **10**   (b) **9**   (c) **16**   (d) **34**

 10 Which is the bigger:
(a) $10^2 + 10$ (b) $9^2 + 20$ (c) $12^2 - 10$ (d) $100 + 4^2$

Quiz 25 score

Using Numbers
QUIZ
26

Q10

 1 Which is longest?
(a) **200 millimetres** (b) **22 centimetres** (c) **220 centimetres** (d) **20 metres**

 2 Continue the sequence … 100, 200, 400, 800, …
(a) **1600** (b) **1000** (c) **3400** (d) **12,000**

 3 How many goals are there on 16 soccer pitches?
(a) **62** (b) **64** (c) **30** (d) **32**

 4 What's the square root of 121?
(a) **9** (b) **10** (c) **11** (d) **242**

 5 What is 1256 ÷ 4?
(a) **216** (b) **300** (c) **314** (d) **324**

 6 Subtract 1509 from 7599
(a) **6090** (b) **6000** (c) **7090** (d) **5590**

 7 Can you answer this chain sum: 5 + 6 +7 − 8?
(a) **16** (b) **10** (c) **29** (d) **26**

Q1

 8 How many even numbers come before 16?
(a) **5** (b) **7** (c) **8** (d) **10**

 9 If x − 500 = 1750, what is x?
(a) **2500** (b) **2230** (c) **2250** (d) **1250**

 10 How old will a person born in 1926 be in 2014?
(a) **76** (b) **78** (c) **88** (d) **108**

Quiz 26 score

Using Numbers QUIZ

27

Q3

 1 Multiply 15.5 x 4
(a) **50**   (b) **40**   (c) **55**   (d) **62**

 2 What's the area of a square 15 x 15 cm?
(a) **200 sq cm**   (b) **225 sq cm**   (c) **300 sq cm**   (d) **350 sq cm**

 3 If 6 female pigs each produce 11 piglets, how many piglets altogether?
(a) **17**   (b) **66**   (c) **72**   (d) **100**

 4 Subtract 55 from 935
(a) **860**   (b) **870**   (c) **875**   (d) **880**

 5 How many 50s in 1900?
(a) **17**   (b) **90**   (c) **38**   (d) **29**

Q6

 6 If Jack is 17 years older than Bill (35) , how old is Jack?
(a) **45**   (b) **52**   (c) **55**   (d) **62**

 7 How many legs on eight crabs?
(a) **16**   (b) **32**   (c) **48**   (d) **80**

 8 What is 5² added to 5²?
(a) **10**   (b) **35**   (c) **50**   (d) **100**

Q9

 9 What's the biggest throw with 2 dice?
(a) **16**   (b) **20**   (c) **12**   (d) **10**

 10 Which sum does not make 144?
(a) **72 + 72**   (b) **288 halved**   (c) **13² – 5²**   (d) **720 – 556**

Quiz 27 score

61

Using Numbers
QUIZ
28

Q2

 1 What's 142,857 x 7?
(a) **1 million**   (b) **100,000**   (c) **999,999**   (d) **777,777**

 2 Born January 1878, died May 1975; how old was this person?
(a) **97**   (b) **73**   (c) **77**   (d) **69**

 3 A cricketer scores 450 runs in 15 innings; what's his average?
(a) **25**   (b) **30**   (c) **40**   (d) **100**

 4 What do you get if you add the top 3 numbers on a calculator (no looking!) ?
(a) **6**   (b) **20**   (c) **24**   (d) **15**

 5 Which maths sign is a shortened form of the Latin *et* (and)?
(a) **–**   (b) **+**   (c) **x**   (d) **÷**

Q10

 6 What is 12.5% of £200?
(a) **£12.50**   (b) **£10**   (c) **£25**   (d) **£15.75**

 7 What is (11 ÷ 10) x 10?
(a) **1**   (b) **10**   (c) **11**   (d) **1.1**

 8 Estimate the weight of 2 elephants
(a) **12,000 kg**   (b) **1000 kg**   (c) **50,000 kg**   (d) **100,000 kg**

 9 What's one-sixth (not exact) as a decimal?
(a) **0.15**   (b) **0.125**   (c) **0.6**   (d) **0.166**

 10 At 800 km/h, how long to fly 10,000 kilometres, and back?
(a) **12 hours**   (b) **15 hours**   (c) **20 hours**   (d) **25 hours**

Quiz 28 score

Chart Your Scores

	1	2	3	4	5	6	7	8	9	10
Quiz 1										
Quiz 2										
Quiz 3										
Quiz 4										
Quiz 5										
Quiz 6										
Quiz 7										
Quiz 8										
Quiz 9										
Quiz 10										
Quiz 11										
Quiz 12										
Quiz 13										
Quiz 14										
Quiz 15										
Quiz 16										
Quiz 17										
Quiz 18										
Quiz 19										
Quiz 20										
Quiz 21										
Quiz 22										
Quiz 23										
Quiz 24										
Quiz 25										
Quiz 26										
Quiz 27										
Quiz 28										

Everyday Science

Key to subject icons

 Technology

 Science at work

 Science at home

 Space

 Machines

 Inventions

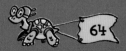

Everyday Science QUIZ

1

Q1

 1 Which needs no electricity?
(a) **TV**   (b) **Computer**   (c) **CD player**   (d) **Balloon**

 2 Which of these of was not a 20th century invention?
(a) **Microwave**   (b) **Jet plane**   (c) **Television**   (d) **Telephone**

Q4

 3 What machine has gears and a cooling system?
(a) **Car**   (b) **Vacuum Cleaner**   (c) **Shaver**   (d) **Washing Machine**

 4 For what invention is Edison most famous?
(a) **Light bulb**   (c) **Machine gun**   (c) **Spacesuit**   (d) **Camera**

 5 Astronauts become … what, in space?
(a) **Painless**   (b) **Breathless**   (c) **Careless**   (d) **Weightless**

 6 The 1940s Gloster Meteor was an early … what?
(a) **Jet plane**   (b) **Spacecraft**   (c) **Guided Missile**   (d) **Robot**

 7 What is the science name for common salt?
(a) **Sulphuric Acid**   (b) **Copper Sulphate**   (c) **Sodium Chloride**
(d) **Hydrogen Sulphide**

Q8

 8 What are the 'maria' on the moon?
(a) **Mountains**   (b) **Seas**   (c) **Flat areas**   (d) **Craters**

 9 What is found in layers called strata?
(a) **Rocks**   (b) **Stars**   (c) **Tree roots**   (d) **Seashells**

 10 Which of these gives radiant energy?
(a) **Electric fire**   (b) **Windmill**   (c) **Bicycle**   (d) **Hydro-electric dam**

Quiz 1 score

Everyday Science QUIZ

2

Q1

 1 Which part of the body is strengthened by fluoride in water?
(a) **Skin**   (b) **Hair**   (c) **Teeth**   (d) **Muscles**

Q3

 2 Which is part of an aircraft?
(a) **Elevator**   (b) **Anchor**   (c) **Drum**   (d) **Gear box**

 3 Which of these is a 'jump jet'?
(a) **Hopper**   (b) **Harrier**   (c) **Hurricane**   (d) **Tornado**

 4 Which letter stands for the gas oxygen?
(a) **H**   (b) **O**   (c) **X**   (d) **N**

 5 What was the famous scientist Newton's first name?
(a) **Isaac**   (b) **Ivor**   (c) **Ian**   (d) **Ike**

 6 Who fell to his death when his wings melted?
(a) **Blanchard**   (b) **Bleriot**   (c) **Wilbur Wright**   (d) **Icarus**

 7 What kind of machines are dirigibles?
(a) **Airships**   (b) **Submarines**   (c) **Cars**   (d) **Computers**

Q4

 8 Which of these is an Internet search engine?
(a) **Goggle**   (b) **Boggle**   (c) **Google**   (d) **Toggle**

 9 Which machine can pierce solid steel, using light?
(a) **Sonar**   (b) **Laser**   (c) **Magnetometer**   (d) **Bessemer converter**

 10 On which ship did Charles Darwin make his historic voyage?
(a) **Terrier**   (b) **Victory**   (c) **Beagle**   (d) **Challenger**

Quiz 2 score

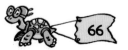

Everyday Science QUIZ

3

Q1

| | | Your answer | Book answer |

1 Which carpentry tool has teeth?
(a) **Saw** (b) **Pincers** (c) **Hammer** (d) **Chisel**

2 What part of a computer shows the picture?
(a) **Monitor** (b) **Minotaur** (c) **Miniature** (d) **Module**

3 Which of these is an element?
(a) **Plastic** (b) **Wood** (c) **Iron** (d) **Air**

4 What did Crick and Watson study in the 1950s?
(a) **BSA** (b) **DNA** (c) **VTOL** (d) **ITV**

Q9

5 Which space probe got lost on Mars?
(a) **Spaniel** (b) **Beagle** (c) **Whippet** (d) **Poodle**

6 What do we call a 'bumpy bit' during an airline flight?
(a) **Oscillation** (b) **Indigestion** (c) **Turbulence** (d) **Deviation**

Q5

7 Which is the odd one out (not seagoing)?
(a) **Catamaran** (b) **Tug** (c) **Yacht** (d) **Paraglider**

8 Plastics are a kind of … what?
(a) **Polymer** (b) **Polygon** (c) **Polynesian** (d) **Polyglot**

9 Which of these runs on 'caterpillar tracks'?
(a) **4 x 4** (b) **Bulldozer** (c) **Bus** (d) **Slow train**

10 Which of these was a pioneer of jet flight?
(a) **De Rozier** (b) **De Havilland** (c) **De Gaulle** (d) **De Montfort**

Quiz 3 score

Everyday Science QUIZ

4

Q3

 1 Which is not a synthetic material?
(a) **PVC**   (b) **Nylon**   (c) **Ice**   (d) **Propene**

 2 What would you use a loom for?
(a) **Weaving**   (b) **Making music**   (c) **Boring Holes**   (d) **Cutting Wood**

 3 Which of these is not a constellation in space?
(a) **Great Bear**   (b) **Serpent**   (c) **Great Cow**   (d) **Orion the Hunter**

 4 Which word means 'driven by air'?   Q5
(a) **Hydraulic**   (b) **Ergonomic**   (c) **Luminous**   (d) **Pneumatic**

 5 Which tool is used to smooth wood?
(a) **Chisel**   (b) **Drill**   (c) **Plane**   (d) **Axe**

 6 How many hulls has a trimaran boat?
(a) **One**   (b) **Two**   (c) **Three**   (d) **Four**

 7 Which is the smallest?   Q8
(a) **Cell**   (b) **Atom**   (c) **Molecule**   (d) **Gram**

 8 Which instrument needs a lens or two?
(a) **Telescope**   (b) **Drill**   (c) **Food mixer**   (d) **Toothbrush**

 9 A ship's speed is measured in … what?
(a) **Bows**   (b) **Gills**   (c) **Knots**   (d) **Tonnes**

 10 An alloy is …?
(a) **A mixture of metals**   (b) **An acid**   (c) **A rock**   (d) **A small planet**

Quiz 4 score

Everyday Science QUIZ

5

Q1

1 Where do aquanauts travel?
(a) **In air**   (b) **In water**   (c) **Underground**   (d) **In space**

2 Who might use Braille?
(a) **Blind people**   (b) **Pilots**   (c) **Doctors**   (d) **Engineers**

3 What sign goes with the positive electrode of an electrical circuit?
(a) **+**   (b) **−**   (c) **%**   (d) *****

4 What is it like inside a kiln?
(a) **Very wet**   (b) **Very cold**   (c) **Very windy**   (d) **Very hot**

5 What joins the wheels of a car?
(a) **Engine**   (b) **Axle**   (c) **Brake cable**   (d) **Exhaust**

6 Which spacecraft travelled around on Mars?
(a) **Apollo**   (b) **Wanderer**   (c) **Sojourner**   (d) **Galileo**

7 Using radio waves to detect faraway objects is called …?
(a) **Radar**   (b) **Sonar**   (c) **Ultra**   (d) **VHF**

Q4

8 Lister, Simpson and Barnard are famous names in which field of science?
(a) **Space**   (b) **Computers**   (c) **Medicine**   (d) **Maths**

9 Which of these are rays from space?
(a) **Gemma**   (b) **Gimme**   (c) **Gamma**   (d) **Gummy**

10 In which century did people first ride on steam trains?
(a) **16th**   (b) **17th**   (c) **18th**   (d) **19th**

Q7

Quiz 5 score

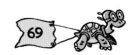

Everyday Science
QUIZ
6

Q1

1 Which word describes communication using thought alone?
(a) **Brainwashing** (b) **Levitation** (c) **Hypnotism** (d) **Telepathy**

2 Where would a doctor find your vertebrae?
(a) **Spine** (b) **Feet** (c) **Stomach** (d) **Skull**

3 Which was the first jet airliner?
(a) **747** (b) **Shooting Star** (c) **V-1** (d) **Comet**

4 Charcoal and diamond are two forms of which element?
(a) **Oxygen** (b) **Carbon** (c) **Iron** (d) **Uranium**

Q8

5 Which machine does not exist?
(a) **Digital camera** (b) **Flat-screen TV** (c) **Invisibility machine**
(d) **Artificial heart**

6 Which would be good for filling a balloon?
(a) **Helium** (b) **Lead** (c) **Sodium** (d) **Calcium**

7 Which machine drops ballast to help it travel higher?
(a) **Airliner** (b) **Balloon** (c) **Rocket** (d) **Car**

Q2

8 Where did Neil Armstrong take a first step in 1969?
(a) **Bottom of the ocean** (b) **Mars** (c) **Moon** (d) **South Pole**

9 What goes with a bolt to make a connection?
(a) **Nut** (b) **Spanner** (c) **Nit** (d) **Wrench**

10 Ada Lovelace was a famous ... what?
(a) **Astronaut** (b) **Chemist** (c) **Mathematician** (d) **Science teacher**

Quiz 6 score

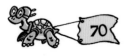

Everyday Science QUIZ

7

Q1

1 Which part of a drill makes the hole?
(a) **Tongue**   (b) **Probe**   (c) **Tooth**   (d) **Bit**

2 Which is a unit of electricity?
(a) **Isobar**   (b) **Watt**   (c) **Degree**   (d) **Centimetre**

3 Weather scientists are called … what?
(a) **Mathematicians**   (b) **Meteorologists**   (c) **Astrologers**
(d) **Futurologists**

Q9

4 What has an icy body and a glowing tail?
(a) **Polar bear**   (b) **Star**   (c) **Comet**   (d) **Volcano**

5 H_2O is the chemical name for which substance?
(a) **Lemonade**   (b) **Milk**   (c) **Water**   (d) **Air**

6 What did Alexander Graham Bell invent?
(a) **Doorbell**   (b) **Telephone**   (c) **Television**   (d) **Computer**

7 What is the correct name for a large space rock?
(a) **Missile**   (b) **Apogee**   (c) **Asteroid**   (d) **Solar flare**

8 Which device is used to give commands to a computer?
(a) **Battery**   (b) **Mouse**   (c) **Microphone**   (d) **Ear-trumpet**

Q5

9 Which of these could be used to start a fire?
(a) **Tuning fork**   (b) **Magnifying glass**   (c) **Ice cube**   (d) **Protractor**

10 Of what were Faraday and Oersted 19th-century pioneers?
(a) **Steam trains**   (b) **Balloons**   (c) **Photography**   (d) **Electricity**

Quiz 7 score

Everyday Science
QUIZ

Q9

 1 What comes out of the spout of a boiling kettle?
(a) **Hydrogen** (b) **Dust** (c) **Steam** (d) **Electricity**

 2 Which was the first 1940s computer?
(a) **ENIAC** (b) **OVERLORD** (c) **DYNAMO** (d) **MENTAL**

 3 Which robots were made famous by the Dr Who TV series?
(a) **Clangers** (b) **Munchers** (c) **Gobblers** (d) **Daleks**

 4 Which craft has rotors for wings?
(a) **Glider** (b) **Helicopter** (c) **Hydrofoil** (d) **Hovercraft**

Q6

 5 Suez and Panama are famous …?
(a) **Bridges** (b) **Tunnels** (c) **Islands** (d) **Canals**

 6 Which rays are used in hospitals to take pictures?
(a) **X-rays** (b) **Z-rays** (c) **Beta rays** (d) **Y-rays**

 7 How many stars form the centre of our solar system?
(a) **None** (b) **One** (c) **Two** (d) **Seven**

 8 A liquid with a solid dissolved in it is a …?
(a) **Element** (b) **Mixture** (c) **Solution** (d) **Compound**

 9 Juice produced by glands in the mouth is …?
(a) **Blood** (b) **Saliva** (c) **Hormones** (d) **Sweat**

Q1

 10 What year did an electric car reach a speed of 63 km/h?
(a) **1800** (b) **1898** (c) **1940** (d) **1985**

Quiz 8 score

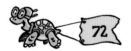

Everyday Science QUIZ

9

Q6

1 The control centre of a submarine is a …?
(a) **Bridge** (b) **Conning tower** (c) **Cockpit** (d) **Command module**

2 A shield to protect the face and eyes is a …?
(a) **Viscount** (b) **Vice** (c) **Visor** (d) **Vitals**

Q2

3 Which kind of engine is used in ships?
(a) **Steam turbine** (b) **Steam iron** (c) **Steam car** (d) **Steam pudding**

4 What year did cars first run on air-filled tyres?
(a) **1895** (b) **1910** (c) **1920** (d) **1936**

5 CCTV is everywhere: what does CC stand for?
(a) **Cunningly Concealed** (b) **Closed Circuit** (c) **Computer Coded**
(d) **Crime Catching**

6 *Rocket* and *Locomotive* were names of early … what?
(a) **Steam locos** (b) **Steamships** (c) **Planes** (d) **Washing machines**

7 What part of a car has an oil filter?
(a) **Steering wheel** (b) **Boot** (c) **Headlight** (d) **Engine**

Q8

8 Who might use a tip action rod?
(a) **Plumber** (b) **Golfer** (c) **Angler** (d) **Snooker player**

9 Which device has a viewfinder?
(a) **Camera** (b) **TV set** (c) **Microwave** (d) **Gun**

10 What is the common name for calcium carbonate?
(a) **Coal** (b) **Soap** (c) **Chalk** (d) **Alcohol**

Quiz 9 score

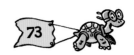

Everyday Science QUIZ

10

Q3

 1 Which is closest to normal body temperature in people?
(a) **0°C**   (b) **37°C**   (c) **100°C**   (d) **250°C**

 2 Which yellowish substance has the symbol S?
(a) **Silicon**   (b) **Silver**   (c) **Sodium**   (d) **Sulphur**

Q6

 3 Who first flew at Kitty Hawk in 1903?
(a) **Wright brothers**   (b) **Lindbergh**   (c) **Montgolfier**   (d) **Brunel**

 4 Silver Ghost is a luxury make of what?
(a) **Television**   (b) **Vacuum cleaner**   (c) **Car**   (d) **Pen**

 5 Which is the Red Planet?
(a) **Venus**   (b) **Mars**   (c) **Saturn**   (d) **Pluto**

Q8

 6 TNT is a kind of what …?
(a) **Disease**   (b) **Explosive**   (c) **Plastic**   (d) **Racing car**

 7 Which is not an alternative energy source?
(a) **Oil**   (b) **Wind**   (c) **Sound**   (d) **Tides**

 8 What do we call a shadow-clock?
(a) **Sunspot**   (b) **Sunshade**   (c) **Sunlamp**   (d) **Sundial**

 9 What travels at 300,000 km a second?
(a) **Heat**   (b) **Jet plane**   (c) **Earth**   (d) **Light**

10 What did Sir Godfrey Hounsfield (1919–2004) invent?
(a) **Car**   (b) **CAT scanner**   (c) **Television**   (d) **Jet engine**

Your answer

Book answer

Quiz 10 score

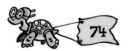

Everyday Science
QUIZ
11

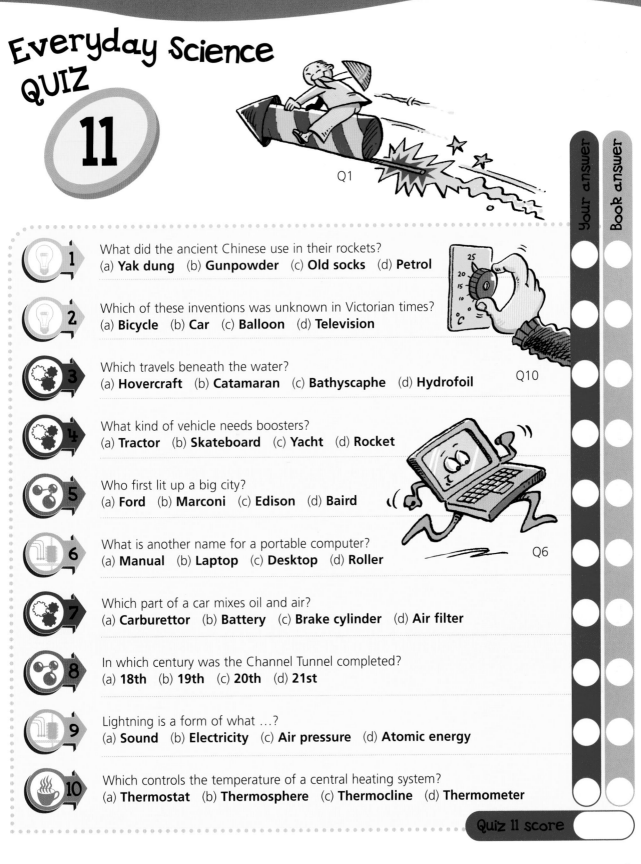

Q1

Q10

Q6

1 What did the ancient Chinese use in their rockets?
(a) **Yak dung** (b) **Gunpowder** (c) **Old socks** (d) **Petrol**

2 Which of these inventions was unknown in Victorian times?
(a) **Bicycle** (b) **Car** (c) **Balloon** (d) **Television**

3 Which travels beneath the water?
(a) **Hovercraft** (b) **Catamaran** (c) **Bathyscaphe** (d) **Hydrofoil**

4 What kind of vehicle needs boosters?
(a) **Tractor** (b) **Skateboard** (c) **Yacht** (d) **Rocket**

5 Who first lit up a big city?
(a) **Ford** (b) **Marconi** (c) **Edison** (d) **Baird**

6 What is another name for a portable computer?
(a) **Manual** (b) **Laptop** (c) **Desktop** (d) **Roller**

7 Which part of a car mixes oil and air?
(a) **Carburettor** (b) **Battery** (c) **Brake cylinder** (d) **Air filter**

8 In which century was the Channel Tunnel completed?
(a) **18th** (b) **19th** (c) **20th** (d) **21st**

9 Lightning is a form of what …?
(a) **Sound** (b) **Electricity** (c) **Air pressure** (d) **Atomic energy**

10 Which controls the temperature of a central heating system?
(a) **Thermostat** (b) **Thermosphere** (c) **Thermocline** (d) **Thermometer**

Your answer

Book answer

Quiz 11 score

Everyday Science QUIZ

12

Q8

 1 What is the hot wire inside a light-bulb called?
(a) **Terminal** (b) **Fuse** (c) **Filament** (d) **Earth**

 2 Who were the first people to use paper?
(a) **Chinese** (b) **Greeks** (c) **Egyptians** (d) **Arabs**

Q1

 3 What would you use to weigh things?
(a) **Microscope** (b) **Scales** (c) **Binoculars** (d) **Tape measure**

 4 What does an oculist examine?
(a) **Your ears** (b) **Your reflexes** (c) **Your lungs** (d) **Your eyes**

 5 What did Chester Carlson invent in the 1940s?
(a) **Photocopier** (b) **Video camera** (c) **Frozen food** (d) **Binoculars**

 6 What is a rubbing force between two things called?
(a) **Friction** (b) **Impact** (c) **Evacuation** (d) **Acceleration**

 7 The ends of a magnet are called … what?
(a) **Roots** (b) **Poles** (c) **Rods** (d) **Pins**

 8 What does an ornithologist study?
(a) **Insects** (b) **Birds** (c) **Fish** (d) **Icicles**

Q7

 9 Which bit in an electric plug 'blows' if the current is too strong?
(a) **Fuse** (b) **Lead** (c) **Core** (d) **Pin**

 10 The study of sound is called …?
(a) **Astronautics** (b) **Ballistics** (c) **Physics** (d) **Acoustics**

Quiz 12 score

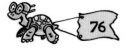

Everyday Science QUIZ

13

Q4

1 *Concorde* was the only successful … what?
(a) **Supersonic airliner**   (b) **Airship**   (c) **Solar bike**   (d) **Jet car**

Q9

2 Which of these women was a scientist?
(a) **Curie**   (b) **Nightingale**   (c) **Borgia**   (d) **Beeton**

3 Which would you probably not find in a science lab?
(a) **Test tube**   (b) **Scales**   (c) **Bunsen burner**   (d) **Metronome**

4 How many tracks has a monorail?
(a) **None**   (b) **One**   (c) **Two**   (d) **Four**

5 With which invention is Elisha Otis linked?
(a) **Lift**   (b) **Rifle**   (c) **Fridge**   (d) **CD**

6 Which transport system used locks and barges?
(a) **Escalator**   (b) **Tube railway**   (c) **Airline**   (d) **Canal**

Q6

7 Which is the fastest of these vehicles?
(a) **Racing car**   (b) **Jet ski**   (c) **Motorbike**   (d) **Satellite**

8 The speed of sound is measured in …?
(a) **Mach numbers**   (b) **Degrees Celsius**   (c) **Kilonewtons**   (d) **Pounds**

9 Which household machine has a drum, a program and hoses?
(a) **Washing machine**   (b) **Microwave**   (c) **Iron**   (d) **Doorbell**

10 What is the first digit (top left) on a telephone keypad?
(a) **0**   (b) **1**   (c) **X**   (d) **10**

Your answer   Book answer

Quiz 13 score

77

Everyday Science QUIZ

14

Q3

Your answer | Book answer

1 AA and AAA are kinds of what …? Q1
(a) **Light bulbs** (b) **Batteries** (c) **Computer programs** (d) **Gases**

2 What makes a toaster work?
(a) **Gas** (b) **Hot air** (c) **Electricity** (d) **Breadcrumbs**

3 Which would be warmest inside?
(a) **Greenhouse** (b) **Garden shed** (c) **Cool box** (d) **Fridge**

4 Which flies through the air?
(a) **Microphone** (b) **Microscope** (c) **Microlight** (d) **Microwave**

5 Who invented a famous miners' safety lamp?
(a) **Raleigh** (b) **Darwin** (c) **Davy** (d) **Newton**

6 Where were the first motorways, called autostradas?
(a) **Germany** (b) **Italy** (c) **Japan** (d) **China**

7 Who invented the engine named after him?
(a) **Benz** (b) **Diesel** (c) **Ford** (d) **Austin**

Q9

8 Kepler and Brahe were two famous … what?
(a) **Painters** (b) **Astronomers** (c) **Explorers** (d) **Soldiers**

9 Jaguar, Mustang and Panda are names of what kinds of machines?
(a) **Cars** (b) **Cleaners** (c) **Computers** (d) **Spacecraft**

10 Which might be a nuclear fuel?
(a) **Gas** (b) **Chalk** (c) **Uranium** (d) **Coal**

Quiz 14 score

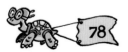

Everyday Science
QUIZ

Q1

 1 C, E and B are all … what?
(a) **Vitamins**   (b) **Diseases**   (c) **Languages**   (d) **Blood types**

 2 Which device always spins steadily?
(a) **Telescope**   (b) **Gyroscope**   (c) **Stethoscope**   (d) **Microscope**

 3 Where would you find the sequence QWERTY?
(a) **Piano**   (b) **Code book**   (c) **Alphabet**   (d) **Keyboard**

 4 Which car company built the Model T of 1908?
(a) **BMW**   (b) **Honda**   (c) **Renault**   (d) **Ford**

 5 In what did a Frenchman named Cugnot ride in 1770?
(a) **Hot air balloon**   (b) **Glider**   (c) **Steam tractor**   (d) **Jet boat**

Q9

 6 Of which technology was Vulcan the god?
(a) **Carpentry**   (b) **Shipbuilding**   (c) **Mining**   (d) **Metalworking**

 7 Which of these people tried to go fast on land and water?
(a) **Donald Campbell**   (b) **Roger Bannister**   (c) **Albert Einstein**
(d) **Linford Christie**

 8 Which planet is ringless?
(a) **Saturn**   (b) **Neptune**   (c) **Jupiter**   (d) **Earth**

 9 Which of these was a medieval science?
(a) **Genetics**   (b) **Alchemy**   (c) **Ultrasonics**   (d) **Nuclear physics**

Q10

 10 What kind of animal was Dolly the clone?
(a) **Chicken**   (b) **Rat**   (c) **Sheep**   (d) **Fish**

Quiz 15 score

Everyday Science
QUIZ

16

Q6

1 What is 'amp' short for?
(a) **Ampion** (b) **Amplitude** (c) **Ampere** (d) **Amplification**

2 What is the chemical symbol for carbon?
(a) **C** (b) **Ca** (c) **Carb** (d) **Cn**

Q7

3 What kind of rain damages building and trees?
(a) **Red rain** (b) **Drizzle** (c) **Acid rain** (d) **Heavy rain**

4 What does AC stand for in electricity?
(a) **All clear** (b) **And connect** (c) **Active circuit** (d) **Alternating current**

5 A thin slice of semi-conducting material is a …?
(a) **Chip** (b) **Chop** (c) **Chunk** (d) **Chomp**

6 What record was set by *Thrust 2*?
(a) **Fastest land vehicle** (b) **Heaviest jet**
(c) **Biggest rocket** (d) **Loudest disco**

Q3

7 Where are the Van Allen Belts?
(a) **In a car** (b) **Around the Earth** (c) **On the Moon** (d) **Underground**

8 System of numbers using 0 and 1 is …?
(a) **Morse code** (b) **Binary code** (c) **A–Z** (d) **Braille**

9 Another word for burning in science is …?
(a) **Ingestion** (b) **Indigestion** (c) **Combustion** (d) **Congestion**

10 Which unit is used to measure radio frequencies?
(a) **Hertz** (b) **Volt** (c) **Litre** (d) **Light-year**

Quiz 16 score

Everyday Science QUIZ

17

Q4

	Your answer	Book answer

1 What does electricity flow round?
(a) **A circle**   (b) **A circus**   (c) **A circuit**   (d) **A circumflex**

2 What do we call stars forming a pattern in space?
(a) **Web**   (b) **Mirage**   (c) **Constellation**   (d) **Nebula**

3 Which living things contain chlorophyll?
(a) **Insects**   (b) **Plants**   (c) **Fungi**   (d) **Snails**

4 The force that pulls an object towards is called …?
(a) **Gravy**   (b) **Levity**   (c) **Greed**   (d) **Gravity**

5 What do scientists call the splitting of an atom?
(a) **Collapse**   (b) **Combination**   (c) **Fission**   (d) **Friction**

Q5

6 If something travels in an ellipse, is it …?
(a) **Circular**   (b) **Egg-shaped**   (c) **Triangular**   (d) **Oblong**

7 Red, green and blue in light are … what?
(a) **Contours**   (b) **Complementary**   (c) **Primary colours**   (d) **Invisible**

8 Scientists call the amount of matter in an object … what?
(a) **Length**   (b) **Area**   (b) **Size**   (d) **Mass**

Q9

9 When a liquid turns to vapour it is called…?
(a) **Evaporation**   (b) **Insulation**   (c) **Conduction**   (d) **Electrolysis**

10 Which company is famous for making aircraft?
(a) **Dyson**   (b) **Compaq**   (c) **Lockheed**   (d) **Sony**

Quiz 17 score

81

Everyday Science QUIZ

18

Q3

1 What is RAM short for?
(a) **Random Access Memory**   (b) **Heaviest jet**   (c) **Biggest rocket**
(d) **Loudest disco**

2 What is formed when a base reacts with an acid?
(a) **Salt**   (b) **Sand**   (c) **Air**   (d) **More acid**

Q7

3 What did King C Gillette invent?
(a) **Fountain pen**   (b) **Hair dryer**   (c) **Vacuum cleaner**   (d) **Safety razor**

4 What might be driven by a linear induction motor?
(a) **Train**   (b) **Computer**   (c) **Car**   (d) **Ship**

5 Space with nothing in it is called … what?
(a) **Ether**   (b) **Vacuum**   (c) **Blankness**   (d) **Nucleus**

6 When light bends it … what?
(a) **Refracts**   (b) **Rejects**   (c) **Multiplies**   (d) **Divides**

7 What transport-linked object has a tread?
(a) **Shoe**   (b) **Tyre**   (c) **Balloon**   (d) **Surfboard**

Q10

8 What do we call a small semi-conducting electronic component?
(a) **Translator**   (b) **Transistor**   (c) **Transporter**   (d) **Transformer**

9 A substance that takes the shape of the container it is in is a …?
(a) **Liquid**   (b) **Compound**   (c) **Solid**   (d) **Mixture**

10 In the 1920s, which scientist built the first liquid-fuelled rockets?
(a) **Einstein**   (b) **Baird**   (c) **Fleming**   (d) **Goddard**

Quiz 18 score

Everyday Science QUIZ

19

Q1

	Your answer	Book answer

 1 Which command tells a PC to turn itself off?
(a) **Get lost**   (b) **Shut down**   (c) **Go away**   (d) **Shut up**

 2 Which of these is a way for heat to travel?
(a) **Compression**   (b) **Conduction**   (c) **Confusion**   (d) **Conflict**

Q5

 3 Which device might have a diaphragm?
(a) **Microphone**   (b) **Television**   (c) **Lawnmower**   (d) **Spectacles**

 4 Where might you find carbon brushes?
(a) **Cupboard**   (b) **Hairdressers**   (c) **Car engine**   (d) **Electric motor**

 5 Which is a kind of needle used in sound recording?
(a) **Stilt**   (b) **Statue**   (c) **Stylus**   (d) **Stiletto**

 6 In which decade was video recording on tape first used?
(a) **1920s**   (b) **1950s**   (c) **1970s**   (d) **1990s**

Q3

 7 What gives pale skins a tan?
(a) **Ultraviolet light**   (b) **Gamma rays**   (c) **Scarlet fever**   (d) **X-rays**

 8 Which is a special kind of solution?
(a) **Steroid**   (b) **Colloid**   (c) **Asteroid**   (d) **Bunion**

 9 Where would a combine harvester be used?
(a) **In a kitchen**   (b) **On a farm**   (c) **In an office**   (d) **In a factory**

 10 In what year was *Sputnik 1* launched into space?
(a) **1907**   (b) **1957**   (c) **1997**   (d) **2007**

Quiz 19 score

Everyday Science
QUIZ
20

Q1

| | | Your answer | Book answer |

 1 Which kitchen utensil acts as a filter?
(a) **Colander** (b) **Cup** (c) **Knife** (d) **Saucepan**

 2 Which object is streamlined?
(a) **Jam jar** (b) **Dart** (c) **Ball** (d) **Parachute**

 3 What would be out of place in an electrical circuit?
(a) **Hammer** (b) **Switch** (c) **Bell** (d) **Bulb**

 4 What must happen for us to hear sound?
(a) **Gyration** (b) **Vibration** (c) **Fixation** (d) **Hydration**

Q5

 5 Which is used by a potter?
(a) **Grid** (b) **Wheel** (c) **Pneumatic drill** (d) **Light pen**

 6 Which would give the highest pitched note?
(a) **Knotted string** (b) **Tight string** (c) **Loose string** (d) **Thick string**

 7 What could not travel through a vacuum chamber?
(a) **X-rays** (b) **Heat** (c) **Light** (d) **Sound**

 8 Which instrument uses two mirrors to look over walls?
(a) **Periscope** (b) **Stethoscope** (c) **Oscilloscope** (d) **Telescope**

 9 Which is the most powerful light source?
(a) **Volcano** (b) **Rainbow** (c) **Sun** (d) **Comet**

 10 Inkjet and laser are two forms of what …?
(a) **Camera** (b) **Printer** (c) **Cooker** (d) **Car engine**

Q8

Quiz 20 score

Everyday Science QUIZ

21

Your answer · Book answer

 1 What is a bar code a set of?
(a) **Colours** (b) **Algebra** (c) **Binary numbers** (d) **Dots**

 2 What would a treasure-hunter or an archaeologist use?
(a) **Metal detector** (b) **Scalpel** (c) **Radiator** (d) **Monkey wrench**

 Q7

3 What does the word 'seismic' have to do with?
(a) **Clouds** (b) **Volcanoes** (c) **Earthquakes** (d) **Ocean waves**

4 What swings inside a mechanical clock?
(a) **Pendulum** (b) **Pen-knife** (c) **Pinwheel** (d) **Crankshaft**

5 What do the letters VHS stand for?
(a) **Very High Standard** (b) **Virtual Home Screen**
(c) **Video Home Recording** (d) **Visual Hand Storage**

6 What do fibre optics systems need?
(a) **Heat** (b) **Light** (c) **Noise** (d) **Dust**

7 What do we call the 'wiggly bit' around a screw?
(a) **Nub** (b) **Cord** (c) **Chuck** (d) **Thread**

8 What part of a ship pushes it along?
(a) **Screw** (b) **Rudder** (c) **Keel** (d) **Anchor**

9 Who might use an endoscope?
(a) **Engineer** (b) **Doctor** (c) **Astronomer** (d) **Film-maker**

Q3

10 What does a lever balance on?
(a) **Fulcrum** (b) **Full stop** (c) **Load** (d) **Angle**

Quiz 21 score

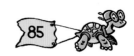

Everyday Science QUIZ

22

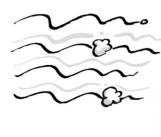

Q1

 1 What kind of land machine can have jib sails?
(a) **Car**   (b) **Barge**   (c) **Windmill**   (d) **Plough**

 2 What device was used to raise water for irrigation in ancient times?
(a) **Catapult**   (b) **Drawbridge**   (c) **Stewpond**   (d) **Shadoof**

 3 Where might you find a leaf spring?
(a) **Truck**   (b) **Greenhouse**   (c) **Watch**   (d) **Telescope**

 4 What is made in a blast furnace?
(a) **Charcoal**   (b) **Steel**   (c) **Plastic**   (d) **Gold**

Q5

 5 What kind of machine is a Chinook?
(a) **Submarine**   (b) **Computer**   (c) **Helicopter**   (d) **Washing machine**

 6 Which household gadget has a condenser and a compressor?
(a) **Cooker**   (b) **Refrigerator**   (c) **Hair dryer**   (d) **Iron**

 7 In what year did the first submarine dive under water?
(a) **1492**   (b) **1776**   (c) **1850**   (d) **1950**

 8 Which of these gadgets uses suction?
(a) **Vacuum cleaner**   (b) **Microwave**   (c) **CD player**   (d) **Telephone**

Q8

 9 Who invented a screw for lifting water from a ditch?
(a) **Da Vinci**   (b) **Archimedes**   (c) **Alexander**   (d) **Columbus**

 10 In which decade was the laser invented?
(a) **1920s**   (b) **1940s**   (c) **1960s**   (d) **1980s**

Quiz 22 score

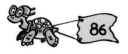

Everyday Science QUIZ

23

Q1

Your answer   **Book answer**

 1 *Columbia* and *Challenger* were the names of … what?
(a) **Ocean Liners**   (b) **Space Shuttles**   (c) **Submarines**   (d) **Computers**

2 What did Sir John Harington sit on in 1589?
(a) **First flush toilet**   (b) **First bicycle**   (c) **First airbed**   (d) **First wheelchair**

 3 What nationality was Galileo?
(a) **Spanish**   (b) **Scottish**   (c) **Greek**   (d) **Italian**

Q5

 4 In 'H-bomb' what does H stand for?
(a) **Horrible**   (b) **Hydrogen**   (b) **Heavy water**   (d) **Helium**

5 What did Hans Lippershey peer through in 1608?
(a) **First glass window**   (b) **First microscope**   (c) **First keyhole**
(d) **First telescope**

 6 What did Jacques Cousteau pioneer?
(a) **Scuba diving gear**   (b) **Jet planes**   (c) **Computers**   (d) **Skis**

7 Where was the first modern oil well drilled in 1859?
(a) **China**   (b) **USA**   (c) **North Sea**   (d) **Saudi Arabia**

8 In which century was the 'modern' screwdriver invented?
(a) **11th**   (b) **16th**   (c) **19th**   (d) **20th**

Q6

9 A 3D image made by laser light is a …?
(a) **Hologram**   (b) **Watercolour**   (c) **Duplicate**   (d) **Photocopy**

10 What is the speed of sound at sea level?
(a) **About 1200 km/h**   (b) **About 500 km/h**   (c) **About 2000 km/h**
(d) **About 5000 km/h**

Quiz 23 score

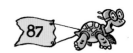

Everyday Science QUIZ

24

Q2

1 With what invention is the name of Marconi linked?
(a) **Vaccination** (b) **Radio** (c) **Telephone** (d) **Electric blanket**

2 What kind of vehicle was a U-boat?
(a) **Hydrofoil** (b) **Speedboat** (c) **Invisible boat** (d) **Submarine**

Q6

3 What do we call the curved surface of a wing?
(a) **Aileron** (b) **Aerofoil** (c) **Undercarriage** (d) **Tailplane**

4 In electronics, what is 'bit' short for?
(a) **Binary digit** (b) **Bit of stuff** (c) **Big number** (d) **Bipole duplicator**

5 What were the 'calculi' used in a Roman abacus for counting?
(a) **Pebbles** (b) **Diamonds** (c) **Dead mice** (d) **Rice grains**

6 Which word describes a monkey's tail that can grip, like a hand?
(a) **Arboreal** (b) **Textile** (c) **Subterranean** (d) **Prehensile**

7 What nationality were Wilbur and Orville Wright?
(a) **South African** (b) **Dutch** (c) **American** (d) **British**

8 Which expands most when heated?
(a) **Gas** (b) **Metal** (c) **Wood** (d) **Milk**

9 What did the Lumière brothers show in the 1890s?
(a) **Films** (b) **X-rays** (c) **Diesel cars** (d) **Gliders**

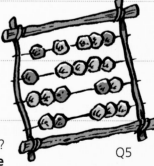

10 What name is given to programs used by a computer?
(a) **Cables** (b) **Keyboard** (c) **Software** (d) **Mouse**

Q5

Quiz 24 score

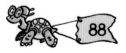

Everyday Science QUIZ

25

Q2

1 Name the point at which light rays meet?
(a) **Feature**   (b) **Hocus**   (c) **Fix**   (d) **Focus**

2 Which is a device for raising heavy weights?
(a) **Jock**   (b) **Jack**   (c) **Tip**   (d) **Vice**

Q10

3 The upward force produced by an aircraft wing is called …?
(a) **Loft**   (b) **Lift**   (c) **Thrust**   (d) **Drag**

4 Which inventor was Scottish?
(a) **Baird**   (b) **Faraday**   (c) **Galvani**   (d) **Tsiolkovski**

5 Which is a machine?
(a) **Block and tackle**   (b) **Sliding Tackle**   (c) **Rugby tackle**
(d) **Chopping block**

6 Which force is applied in the clutch of a car?
(a) **Suction**   (b) **Friction**   (c) **Acceleration**   (d) **Inertia**

Q9

7 What keeps a ship steady in a rough sea?
(a) **Compass**   (b) **Keel**   (c) **Mast**   (d) **Stabilizers**

8 When did people first use ploughs?
(a) **About 10,000BC** (b) **About 20,000BC**   (c) **About 3500BC**
(d) **About AD500**

9 Which is used to measure temperature?
(a) **Weighing scales**   (b) **Thermometer**   (c) **Digital clock**   (d) **Ruler**

10 Which machine has a trolley and a hoist?
(a) **Washing machine**   (b) **X-ray machine**   (c) **Lift**   (d) **Crane**

Quiz 25 score

Everyday Science QUIZ

26

Q6

1 What nationality was James Watt, the steam engine man …?
(a) **American** (b) **Irish** (c) **Scottish** (d) **French**

2 On what did Andre Garnerin float down in 1797?
(a) **Airbed** (b) **Slide** (c) **Snowboard** (d) **Parachute**

Q2
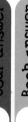

3 What tool is used to 'turn' or shape the round legs of chairs?
(a) **Hammer** (b) **Drill** (c) **Lathe** (d) **Pliers**

4 In which century did people first cook in gas ovens?
(a) **19th** (b) **17th** (c) **15th** (d) **10th**

5 What are a submarine's ballast tanks filled with when submerged?
(a) **Air** (b) **Oil** (c) **Water** (d) **Sand**

6 What kind of machine is an oar?
(a) **Lever** (b) **Wheel** (c) **Pulley** (d) **Screw**

7 Who first printed books using wooden blocks?
(a) **Vikings** (b) **Chinese** (c) **Incas** (d) **Spanish**

8 What shape was the first record (1877)?
(a) **Square** (b) **Round** (c) **Cylinder** (d) **Triangle**

Q9

9 What was *Telstar*, launched in 1962?
(a) **Ship** (b) **Communications satellite** (c) **Electric car**
(d) **Home computer**

10. What did Reginald Fessenden do, a first in 1906?
(a) **Fly** (b) **Waterski** (c) **Broadcast talk radio** (d) **Show TV pictures**

Quiz 26 score

Everyday Science QUIZ

27

Q4

1 Where might you find a toolbar?
(a) **Plumber's van**   (b) **Computer screen**   (c) **Garden shed**   (d) **Car boot**

2 Which is the scientist of these four?
(a) **Dramatist**   (b) **Physicist**   (c) **Gymnast**   (d) **Activist**

3 Which is not a shape?
(a) **Cube**   (b) **Pentagon**   (c) **Sphere**   (d) **Bongoid**

Q10

4 Which of these is not a health risk?
(a) **Fresh air**   (b) **Smoking**   (c) **Obesity**   (d) **Alcohol**

5 Which science word means 'bendy'?
(a) **Flat**   (b) **Corrosive**   (c) **Flexible**   (d) **Dehydrated**

6 Which of these is not a solid?
(a) **Chocolate**   (b) **Butter**   (c) **Ice**   (d) **Hydrogen**

7 Which computer command would you use to restore a deletion?
(a) **Undo**   (d) **Don't do**   (c) **Return**   (d) **Quit**

8 Which scientist discovered radio waves in 1888?
(a) **Marconi**   (b) **Edison**   (c) **Zworkykin**   (d) **Hertz**

9 In 1714, who first used a mercury thermometer?
(a) **Newton**   (b) **Lavoisier**   (c) **Fahrenheit**   (d) **Faraday**

Q9

10 A log roller under a heavy stone was an ancient form of what …?
(a) **Lubricant**   (b) **Bearing**   (c) **Brake**   (d) **Jack**

Quiz 27 score

Everyday Science QUIZ

28

Q1

Your answer | **Book answer**

1. Where would you find a Plimsoll mark?
(a) **On trainers** (b) **On a ship** (c) **In a bath** (d) **On a medicine bottle**

2. What kind of wire is inside an electrical flex?
(a) **Gold** (b) **Copper** (c) **Silver** (d) **Lead**

3. Which is not a good thermal insulator?
(a) **Cork** (b) **Wood** (c) **Plastic** (d) **Steel**

Q6

4. Which mechanical device has an escapement?
(a) **Electric toothbrush** (b) **Lift** (c) **Baby buggy** (d) **Clock**

5. A sloping surface is a … what?
(a) **Inclined plane** (b) **Aeroplane** (c) **Isosceles triangle** (d) **Tangent**

6. Toothed wheels that interlock are called … what?
(a) **Springs** (b) **Gears** (c) **Bevels** (d) **Cams**

7. What does a damper do in a machine?
(a) **Absorbs moisture** (b) **Lubricates** (c) **Absorbs vibration**
(d) **Creates vibration**

8. In which decade did people first see a form of TV?
(a) **1920s** (b) **1940s** (c) **1950s** (d) **1960s**.

Q5

9. Which device stores energy in a friction-drive toy?
(a) **Cartwheel** (b) **Gearwheel** (c) **Flywheel** (d) **Dynamo**

10. Launched in 1954, the *Nautilus* was the first …?
(a) **Rocket** (b) **Nuclear submarine** (c) **Cruise missile** (d) **Turbine car**

Quiz 28 score

Chart Your Scores

	1	2	3	4	5	6	7	8	9	10
Quiz 1										
Quiz 2										
Quiz 3										
Quiz 4										
Quiz 5										
Quiz 6										
Quiz 7										
Quiz 8										
Quiz 9										
Quiz 10										
Quiz 11										
Quiz 12										
Quiz 13										
Quiz 14										
Quiz 15										
Quiz 16										
Quiz 17										
Quiz 18										
Quiz 19										
Quiz 20										
Quiz 21										
Quiz 22										
Quiz 23										
Quiz 24										
Quiz 25										
Quiz 26										
Quiz 27										
Quiz 28										

General Knowledge

Key to subject icons

 Geography

 Everyday life

 History

 People

 Science

 Nature

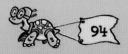

General Knowledge QUIZ

1

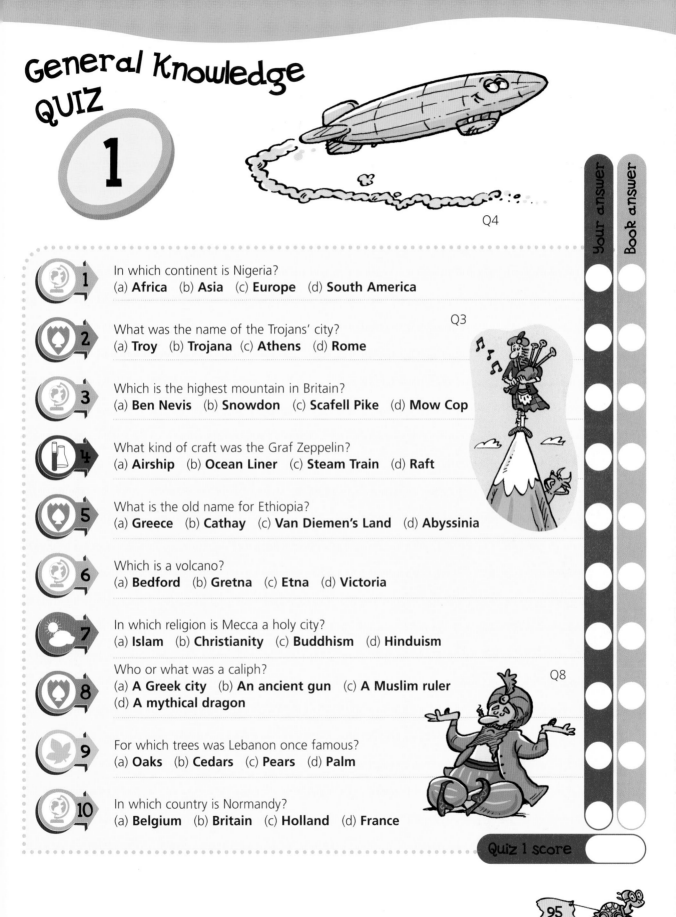

Q4

1 In which continent is Nigeria?
(a) **Africa**   (b) **Asia**   (c) **Europe**   (d) **South America**

2 What was the name of the Trojans' city?
(a) **Troy**   (b) **Trojana**   (c) **Athens**   (d) **Rome**

Q3

3 Which is the highest mountain in Britain?
(a) **Ben Nevis**   (b) **Snowdon**   (c) **Scafell Pike**   (d) **Mow Cop**

4 What kind of craft was the Graf Zeppelin?
(a) **Airship**   (b) **Ocean Liner**   (c) **Steam Train**   (d) **Raft**

5 What is the old name for Ethiopia?
(a) **Greece**   (b) **Cathay**   (c) **Van Diemen's Land**   (d) **Abyssinia**

6 Which is a volcano?
(a) **Bedford**   (b) **Gretna**   (c) **Etna**   (d) **Victoria**

7 In which religion is Mecca a holy city?
(a) **Islam**   (b) **Christianity**   (c) **Buddhism**   (d) **Hinduism**

8 Who or what was a caliph?
(a) **A Greek city**   (b) **An ancient gun**   (c) **A Muslim ruler**
(d) **A mythical dragon**

Q8

9 For which trees was Lebanon once famous?
(a) **Oaks**   (b) **Cedars**   (c) **Pears**   (d) **Palm**

10 In which country is Normandy?
(a) **Belgium**   (b) **Britain**   (c) **Holland**   (d) **France**

Quiz 1 score

General Knowledge QUIZ

2

Q1

| | | Your answer | Book answer |

1 Which ancient Italian city did a volcano bury?
(a) **St. Albans** (b) **Vienna** (c) **Cairo** (d) **Pompeii**

2 How many wives did Henry VIII have?
(a) **3** (b) **4** (c) **6** (d) **8**

3 Who wasn't a Wild West gunslinger?
(a) **Billy the Kid** (b) **Wyatt Earp** (c) **Sundance Kid** (d) **Garibaldi**

4 Who would have worn chaps?
(a) **A sailor** (b) **A Roman soldier** (c) **A cowboy** (d) **A knight**

5 Where are tortillas a popular food?
(a) **China** (b) **Mexico** (c) **Egypt** (d) **Ireland**

Q7

6 In which continent is the Grand Canyon?
(a) **North America** (b) **Europe** (c) **Africa** (d) **Asia**

7 Which word means 'fear of spiders'?
(a) **Arachnophobia** (b) **Leggyphobia** (c) **Claustrophobia** (d) **Vertigo**

8 Which isn't a lake?
(a) **Geneva** (b) **Lucerne** (c) **Titicaca** (d) **Thames**

Q4

9 Which isn't a root vegetable?
(a) **Potato** (b) **Turnip** (c) **Carrot** (d) **Broccoli**

10 On which mountain is Noah's Ark said to have landed?
(a) **Ararat** (b) **Rushmore** (c) **Everest** (d) **Mont Blanc**

Quiz 2 score

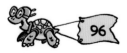

General Knowledge QUIZ

3

Q6

	Your answer	Book answer

1. Where are dwarf trees, or bonsai, grown?
   (a) **Japan**   (b) **Sweden**   (c) **USA**   (d) **Argentina**

2. The Nile is Africa's longest… what?
   (a) **Road**   (b) **River**   (c) **Snake**   (d) **Lake**

3. Which country was ruled by Stalin?
   (a) **China**   (b) **Germany**   (c) **Ireland**   (d) **Russia**

Q4

4. How many reigning British queens have been called Elizabeth?
   (a) **1**   (b) **2**   (c) **3**   (d) **4**

5. How many players make up a rugby union team?
   (a) **11**   (b) **14**   (c) **15**   (d) **22**

6. Who lost the Battle of Bosworth?
   (a) **Robin Hood**   (b) **Harold II**   (c) **Charles I**   (d) **Richard III**

7. In which country are the Mountains of Mourne?
   (a) **Scotland**   (b) **Spain**   (c) **France**   (d) **Ireland**

Q9

8. Who 'singed the King of Spain's beard' in Tudor times?
   (a) **Drake**   (b) **Shakespeare**   (c) **Howard**   (d) **Marlowe**

9. Who was the Norse god of thunder?
   (a) **Osiris**   (b) **Baal**   (c) **Thor**   (d) **Mercury**

10. In which country is the Alhambra?
    (a) **Spain**   (b) **Morocco**   (c) **Mexico**   (d) **Russia**

Quiz 3 score

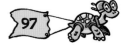

General Knowledge QUIZ

4

Q9

 1 Who might use a particle accelerator?
(a) **Atom scientist** (b) **Cyclist** (c) **Astronaut** (d) **Chef**

 2 Which city is known as the Big Apple?
(a) **Nice** (b) **Naples** (c) **Northampton** (d) **New York**

 3 In which book does Long John Silver appear?
(a) *Treasure Island* (b) *Kidnapped* (c) *Moby Dick* (d) *The Lord of the Rings*

 4 Which of these isn't a make of car?
(a) **Renault** (b) **Ford** (c) **Boeing** (d) **Volvo**

Q3

 5 What's a French castle called?
(a) **Manor** (b) **Chateau** (c) **Dungeon** (d) **Auberge**

 6 Which of these was a poet?
(a) **Tennyson** (b) **Livingstone** (c) **Newton** (d) **Edison**

 7 What score is 'double top' in darts?
(a) **40** (b) **60** (c) **100** (d) **180**

 8 Which of these is an area of flat land?
(a) **Cavern** (b) **Grotto** (c) **Plateau** (d) **Fiord**

 9 What kind of animal is an aye-aye?
(a) **Mammal** (b) **Bird** (c) **Fish** (d) **Reptile**

Q1

 10 Where did Kublai Khan rule?
(a) **China** (b) **South Africa** (c) **India** (d) **Iraq**

Quiz 4 score

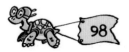

General Knowledge QUIZ

5

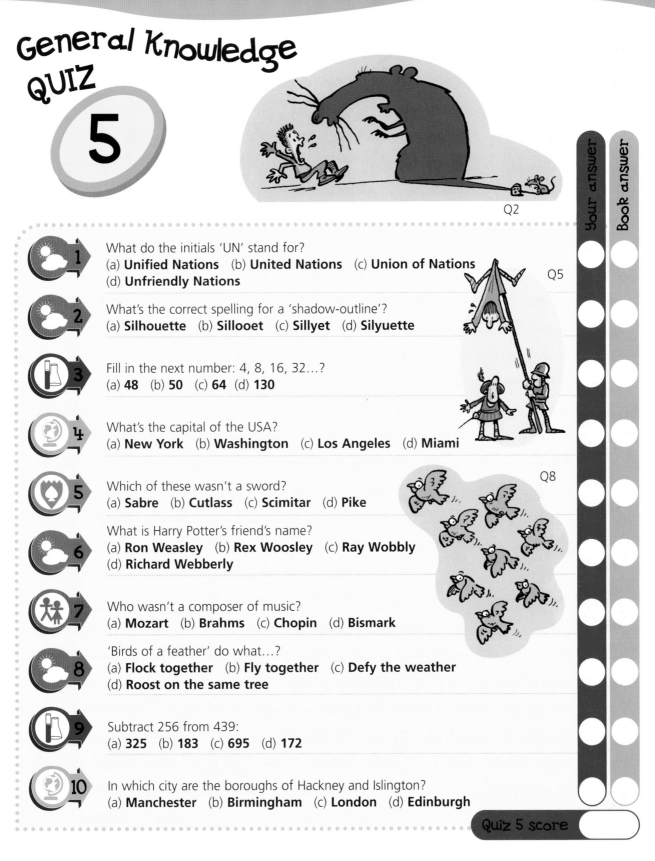

Q2

Q5

Q8

Your answer

Book answer

1 What do the initials 'UN' stand for?
(a) **Unified Nations**   (b) **United Nations**   (c) **Union of Nations**
(d) **Unfriendly Nations**

2 What's the correct spelling for a 'shadow-outline'?
(a) **Silhouette**   (b) **Sillooet**   (c) **Sillyet**   (d) **Silyuette**

3 Fill in the next number: 4, 8, 16, 32…?
(a) **48**   (b) **50**   (c) **64**   (d) **130**

4 What's the capital of the USA?
(a) **New York**   (b) **Washington**   (c) **Los Angeles**   (d) **Miami**

5 Which of these wasn't a sword?
(a) **Sabre**   (b) **Cutlass**   (c) **Scimitar**   (d) **Pike**

6 What is Harry Potter's friend's name?
(a) **Ron Weasley**   (b) **Rex Woosley**   (c) **Ray Wobbly**
(d) **Richard Webberly**

7 Who wasn't a composer of music?
(a) **Mozart**   (b) **Brahms**   (c) **Chopin**   (d) **Bismark**

8 'Birds of a feather' do what…?
(a) **Flock together**   (b) **Fly together**   (c) **Defy the weather**
(d) **Roost on the same tree**

9 Subtract 256 from 439:
(a) **325**   (b) **183**   (c) **695**   (d) **172**

10 In which city are the boroughs of Hackney and Islington?
(a) **Manchester**   (b) **Birmingham**   (c) **London**   (d) **Edinburgh**

Quiz 5 score

General Knowledge QUIZ

6

Q5

Q9

1 'A faint heart never won…' what?
(a) **Fair lady** (b) **A battle** (c) **The race** (d) **Fat stomach**

2 Which of these wasn't a sailor?
(a) **Frobisher** (b) **Wellington** (c) **Jellicoe** (d) **Chichester**

3 Which 'rock' is close to Spain?
(a) **Gibraltar** (b) **Montserrat** (c) **Ascension Island** (d) **Japan**

4 What did Samuel Pepys write?
(a) **A cookery book** (b) **A diary** (c) **A thriller** (d) **An encyclopedia**

5 Complete the proverb: 'a fool and his money…':
(a) **Are soon parted** (b) **Never go far** (c) **Have a good time**
(d) **Are good mates**

6 Name Shakespeare's *Merchant of Venice*:
(a) **Sherlock** (b) **Diplock** (c) **Necklock** (d) **Shylock**

7 Who was the first Tudor monarch?
(a) **Richard III** (b) **Henry VIII** (c) **Henry VII** (d) **Elizabeth I**

8 What is double 5500?
(a) **10,000** (b) **10,500** (c) **11,000** (d) **55,000**

9 Who might have ridden a penny-farthing?
(a) **A Victorian** (b) **A Tudor** (c) **A Roman** (d) **A Viking**

10 Who built the Antonine Wall in Scotland?
Q4
(a) **Picts** (b) **Jacobites** (c) **Celts** (d) **Romans**

Quiz 6 score

General Knowledge QUIZ

7

Q4

		Your answer	Book answer

1 What is the Roman number 5?
(a) **X**   (b) **I**   (c) **0**   (d) **V**

2 Which Briton won two gold medals at the 2004 Athens Olympics?
(a) **Mathew Pinsent**   (b) **Kelly Holmes**   (c) **Amir Khan**   (d) **Paula Radcliffe**

3 Who was King Arthur's wife?
(a) **Merlin**   (b) **Guinevere**   (c) **Morgana**   (d) **Lancelot**

4 Which sport takes place at Henley-on-Thames?
(a) **Rowing**   (b) **Skiing**   (c) **Fishing**   (d) **Swan-racing**

5 What was scary about the mythical Hydra?
(a) **It had 9 heads**   (b) **It had 50 legs**   (c) **It lived in fire**
(d) **It was invisible**

Q5

6 Spell the drink made from apples:
(a) **Cidah**   (b) **Cider**   (c) **Sider**   (d) **Syder**

7 Who was the hero of the film *Braveheart*?
(a) **William Wallace**   (b) **Rob Roy**   (c) **Ben Hur**   (d) **Tarzan**

8 Which insect carries the disease malaria?
(a) **Ant**   (b) **Grasshopper**   (c) **Butterfly**   (d) **Mosquito**

9 What has 'ultrasonics' got to do with?
(a) **Sound**   (b) **Water**   (c) **Light**   (d) **X-rays**

Q8

10 In which country do people speak Mandarin?
(a) **Japan**   (b) **India**   (c) **China**   (d) **Australia**

Quiz 7 score

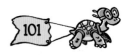

General Knowledge QUIZ

8

Q6

 1 Which of these isn't a metal?
(a) **Tin**   (b) **Copper**   (c) **Hydrogen**   (d) **Gold**

 2 What is a sperm whale's favourite food?
(a) **Squid**   (b) **Penguin**   (c) **Plankton**   (d) **Seaweed**

Q3

3 What kind of craft might be delta-winged?
(a) **Racing car**   (b) **Hydrofoil**   (c) **Aeroplane**   (d) **Submarine**

 4 Who led the 1381 Peasant's Revolt?
(a) **Jack the Ripper**   (b) **Little John**   (c) **Wat Tyler**   (d) **Robert the Bruce**

 5 Who sailed to find the Golden Fleece?
(a) **Joshua**   (b) **Jeremiah**   (c) **Jonah**   (d) **Jason**

 6 Who rode a horse called Black Bess?
(a) **Frankie Dettori**   (b) **Dick Turpin**   (c) **Spiderman**
(d) **Blackbeard the Pirate**

 7 Add (4 x 3) and (3 x 6):
(a) **16**   (b) **21**   (c) **30**   (d) **4336**

Q9

 8 What do geologists study?
(a) **Games**   (b) **Rocks**   (c) **Horses**   (d) **Stars**

 9 What nationality was the painter Picasso?
(a) **Greek**   (b) **Spanish**   (c) **German**   (d) **American**

 10 Where are a grasshopper's ears?
(a) **Mouth**   (b) **Bottom**   (c) **Legs**   (d) **Wings**

Quiz 8 score

General Knowledge QUIZ

9

Q7

1 What is 39 ÷ 3?
(a) **13** (b) **42** (c) **12** (d) **9**

2 Who is the archer-elf in *The Lord of the Rings*?
(a) **Gimli** (b) **Gollum** (c) **Bilbo** (d) **Legolas**

Q2

3 Which of these is a popular TV series?
(a) **Enemies** (b) **Friends** (c) **Rivals** (d) **Chums**

4 In which city is the district called Montmartre?
(a) **London** (b) **Edinburgh** (c) **Paris** (d) **New York**

5 What kind of animal is a hammerhead?
(a) **Beetle** (b) **Woodpecker** (c) **Shark** (d) **Dog**

6 Who shot an apple off his son's head?
(a) **William Tell** (b) **Superman** (c) **Robin Hood** (d) **Kit Corson**

7 Which trees have conkers?
(a) **Horse chestnut** (b) **Ash** (c) **Sycamore** (d) **Oak**

Q5

8 In which country is Natal?
(a) **France** (b) **Canada** (c) **USA** (d) **South Africa**

9 What do we call a mixture of rain and snow?
(a) **Sleet** (b) **Fog** (c) **Drizzle** (d) **Blizzard**

10 Which country was once ruled by the shah?
(a) **Germany** (b) **China** (c) **Iran** (d) **Russia**

Quiz 9 score

General Knowledge QUIZ

10

Q3

1 Who wrote *Oliver Twist*?
(a) **Charles Dickens**   (b) **Lionel Bart**   (c) **Victor Hugo**   (d) **Tim Rice**

2 If someone is 'pallid', they are... what?
(a) **Dead**   (b) **Very ill**   (c) **Pale**   (d) **Mean**

Q6

3 Which of these animals is not spotted?
(a) **Leopard**   (b) **Dalmatian**   (c) **Ocelot**   (d) **Tiger**

4 Which isn't a beetle?
(a) **Ladybird**   (b) **Scarab**   (c) **Devil's coach horse**   (d) **Earwig**

5 Which of these pretends to be someone else?
(a) **Rebel**   (b) **Imposter**   (c) **Tyrant**   (d) **Crook**

6 Who is the literary wizard?
(a) **Hawkeye**   (b) **Gandalf**   (c) **Godolphin**   (d) **Hemlock**

7 A kind of grey rock that splits easily:
(a) **Gold**   (b) **Slate**   (c) **Granite**   (d) **Marble**

Q1

8 A game with numbers on a card:
(a) **Bash**   (b) **Barge**   (c) **Bulge**   (d) **Bingo**

9 Which of these was a famous Greek scientist?
(a) **Bacon**   (b) **Aristotle**   (c) **Brutus**   (d) **Robespierre**

10 Which might be found on a ship?
(a) **Binnacle**   (b) **Pinnacle**   (c) **Cranium**   (d) **Spiracle**

Quiz 10 score

General Knowledge QUIZ

11

Q7

 1 Which Greek hero rode a winged horse?
(a) **Achilles** (b) **Perseus** (c) **Hercules** (d) **Alexander**

 2 Spell the ancient fish:
(a) **Coelacanth** (b) **Sealacan** (c) **Sellocanth** (d) **Ceelyocamp**

 3 What's another word for 'a woven picture'?
(a) **Pastry** (b) **Fretwork** (c) **Mosaic** (d) **Tapestry**

 4 Spell the flower:
(a) **Dahlia** (b) **Daylia** (c) **Dayleeya** (d) **Daelia**

 5 Which king burnt the cakes?
(a) **Canute** (b) **Alfred** (c) **Henry** (d) **Richard**

Q2

 6 Who built the steamship *Great Eastern*?
(a) **Watt** (b) **Raleigh** (c) **Gladstone** (d) **Brunel**

 7 A red sky at night is… what?
(a) **A remarkable sight** (b) **A fireman's fright** (c) **Seldom**
(d) **A shepherd's delight**

 8 What is nearest to 1/3 as a decimal quantity?
(a) **0.33** (b) **0.25** (c) **0.50** (d) **0.75**

 9 What's the masculine for 'sow'?
(a) **Boar** (b) **Ram** (c) **Stag** (d) **Bull**

 10 After which Roman god is March named?
(a) **Mercury** (b) **Mars** (c) **Jupiter** (d) **Apollo**

Quiz 11 score

General Knowledge QUIZ

12

Q1

 1 Which naval ship is the biggest?
(a) **Aircraft carrier**   (b) **Destroyer**   (c) **Submarine**   (d) **Frigate**

 2 Which is wrongly spelt?
(a) **Favourite**   (b) **Comical**   (c) **Tradgedy**   (d) **Opposite**

 3 Which shape has 12 faces?
(a) **Dodecahedron**   (b) **Pentagon**   (c) **Octagon**   (d) **Triangle**

 4 What's over the fireplace?
(a) **Mantelpiece**   (b) **Gutter**   (c) **Coving**   (d) **Floorboard**

Q6

 5 What's the capital of Hungary?
(a) **Belgrade**   (b) **Vienna**   (c) **Budapest**   (d) **Berlin**

 6 How many legs has a tarantula?
(a) **4**   (b) **6**   (c) **8**   (d) **10**

 7 What is 12 x 12?
(a) **100**   (b) **96**   (c) **144**   (d) **248**

 8 Which country was ruled by Mussolini in the 1930s?
(a) **France**   (b) **Italy**   (c) **USA**   (d) **Germany**

 9 Another name for a wildebeest is... what?
(a) **Gnu**   (b) **Giraffe**   (c) **Hyena**   (d) **Griffin**

Q9

 10 What is the Red Ensign?
(a) **A country**   (b) **A flag**   (c) **A badge**   (d) **A secret society**

Quiz 12 score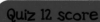

General Knowledge QUIZ

13

Q9

Q1

	Your answer	Book answer

 1 Which item of clothing is named after a lordly general?
(a) **Cardigan** (b) **T-shirt** (c) **Vest** (d) **Jumper**

 2 What colour is the River Danube, according to a tune?
(a) **Red** (b) **Green** (c) **Golden** (d) **Blue**

 3 Where is the Black Forest?
(a) **Canada** (b) **Russia** (c) **Scotland** (d) **Germany**

 4 What is America's Purple Heart?
(a) **A medal** (b) **A flower** (c) **A song** (d) **A state**

 5 Which isn't a flower?
(a) **Hollyhock** (b) **Foxglove** (c) **Buttercup** (d) **Daisywheel**

 6 What colour is the United Nations flag?
(a) **Green** (b) **Red** (c) **Black** (d) **Blue**

 7 Spell a kind of crash:
(a) **Collusion** (b) **Collision** (c) **Collition** (d) **Collyshun**

Q8

 8 What kind of weapon was a flintlock?
(a) **Bow** (b) **Spear** (c) **Sword** (d) **Gun**

 9 Spell the prehistoric animal correctly:
(a) **Triceratops** (b) **Trycherryops** (c) **Treeserrytops** (d) **Triseritops**

 10 Who were the supporters of Bonnie Prince Charlie?
(a) **Jacobins** (b) **Levellers** (c) **Jacobites** (d) **Scallywags**

Quiz 13 score

General Knowledge QUIZ

14

Q3

 1 Spell the musical instrument:
(a) **Saxafone** (b) **Sacksafone** (c) **Saxophone** (d) **Sachsaphone**

 2 What word means 'dried up'?
(a) **Dessicated** (b) **Masticated** (c) **Elasticated** (d) **Serrated**

 3 What kind of machine was the Lancaster?
(a) **WWII bomber** (b) **Steamship** (c) **1880s car** (d) **Space satellite**   Q6

 4 How many 70s in 350?
(a) **3** (b) **5** (c) **6** (d) **9**

5 Spell the capital of Denmark, in English:
(a) **Koppenhaken** (b) **Cooponhargon** (c) **Copenhagen**
(d) **Kopenhaagen**

 6 What's the south American relative of the hippopotamus?
(a) **Jaguar** (b) **Rhea** (c) **Tapir** (d) **Anteater**

 7 What is the square root of 100?
(a) **10** (b) **1000** (c) **150** (d) **110**

 8 Which was a sea battle?
(a) **Hastings** (b) **Jutland** (c) **Alamein** (d) **Stalingrad**

 9 Who flew the Jolly Roger flag?
(a) **Vikings** (b) **Pirates** (c) **Smugglers** (d) **Explorers**   Q9

 10 Which of these was not a British Prime Minister?
(a) **Lloyd George** (b) **Thatcher** (c) **Butler** (d) **Major**

Quiz 14 score

 108

General Knowledge QUIZ

15

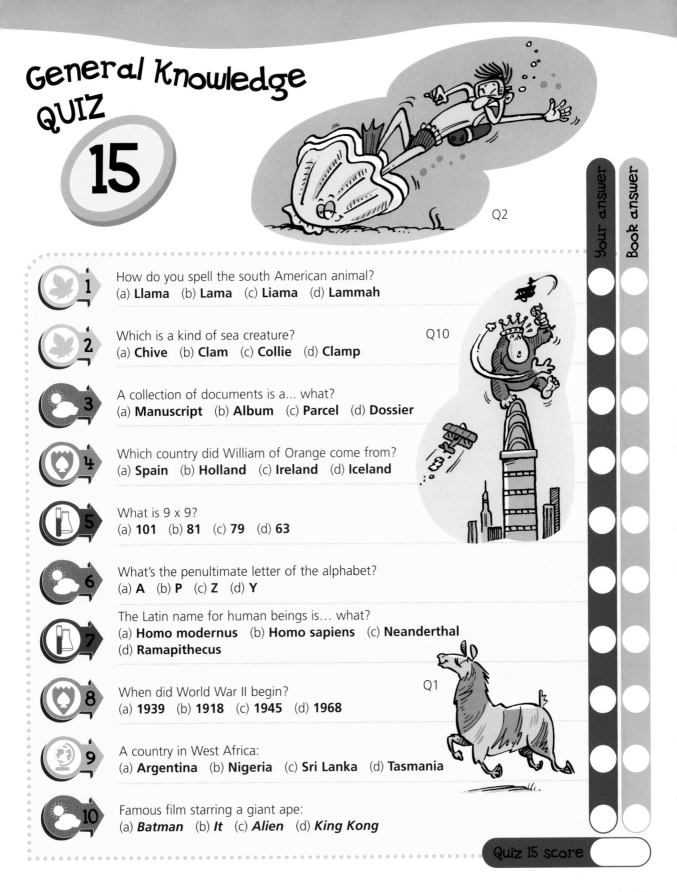

Q2

		Your answer	Book answer

1. How do you spell the south American animal?
   (a) **Llama**   (b) **Lama**   (c) **Liama**   (d) **Lammah**

2. Which is a kind of sea creature?   Q10
   (a) **Chive**   (b) **Clam**   (c) **Collie**   (d) **Clamp**

3. A collection of documents is a... what?
   (a) **Manuscript**   (b) **Album**   (c) **Parcel**   (d) **Dossier**

4. Which country did William of Orange come from?
   (a) **Spain**   (b) **Holland**   (c) **Ireland**   (d) **Iceland**

5. What is 9 x 9?
   (a) **101**   (b) **81**   (c) **79**   (d) **63**

6. What's the penultimate letter of the alphabet?
   (a) **A**   (b) **P**   (c) **Z**   (d) **Y**

7. The Latin name for human beings is… what?
   (a) **Homo modernus**   (b) **Homo sapiens**   (c) **Neanderthal**
   (d) **Ramapithecus**

8. When did World War II begin?   Q1
   (a) **1939**   (b) **1918**   (c) **1945**   (d) **1968**

9. A country in West Africa:
   (a) **Argentina**   (b) **Nigeria**   (c) **Sri Lanka**   (d) **Tasmania**

10. Famous film starring a giant ape:
    (a) *Batman*   (b) *It*   (c) *Alien*   (d) *King Kong*

Quiz 15 score

General Knowledge QUIZ

16

Your answer

Book answer

1 Which is a kind of mineral?
(a) **Soap** (b) **Cheese** (c) **Talc** (d) **Wood**

Q7

2 How many sides has a quadrilateral?
(a) **1** (b) **2** (c) **3** (d) **4**

3 Molten rock from inside a volcano is called… what?
(a) **Magnolia** (b) **Magnet** (c) **Magma** (d) **Magnesium**

4 A kind of deer:
(a) **Elk** (b) **Ermine** (c) **Eel** (d) **Eider**

Q4

5 Who invented a machine called the Spinning Jenny?
(a) **Stephenson** (b) **Einstein** (c) **Hargreaves** (d) **Pitt**

6 Which word means 'to do with the sea'?
(a) **Astral** (b) **Marine** (c) **Stellar** (d) **Globular**

7 A car with a hinged, sloping back:
(a) **Halftrack** (b) **Hatchback** (c) **Saloon** (d) **Sports car**

8 Language spoken by Jewish people:
(a) **Gujarati** (b) **Gaelic** (c) **Breton** (d) **Hebrew**

9 How deep can a whale dive?
(a) **About 10 m** (b) **About 100 m** (c) **About 1000 m** (d) **About 10,000 m**

10 In which city is the Empire State Building?
(a) **Paris** (b) **Berlin** (c) **London** (d) **New York**

Quiz 16 score

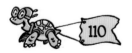

General Knowledge QUIZ

17

Q4

1 A general whose nickname was 'Ike':
(a) **Eisenhower** (b) **Montgomery** (c) **Wellington** (d) **Marlborough**

2 Which US naval base was attacked in 1941?
(a) **Gold Bay** (b) **Emerald Isle** (c) **Pearl Harbor** (d) **Silver Beach**

3 Green cloth used on snooker tables:
(a) **Quilting** (b) **Worsted** (c) **Baize** (d) **Gingham**

Q7

4 Which sea animal has curving tusks?
(a) **Turtle** (b) **Penguin** (c) **Dolphin** (d) **Walrus**

5 What kind of living thing is a bristlecone?
(a) **Tree** (b) **Snake** (c) **Mollusc** (d) **Insect**

6 Melamine, vinyl and polyethylene are all…what?
(a) **Foods** (b) **Stars** (c) **Metals** (d) **Plastics**

7 What a knight carried on one arm:
(a) **Gauntlet** (b) **Helm** (c) **Shield** (d) **Breastplate**

Q3

8 Where on a plane are its ailerons?
(a) **Wings** (b) **Tail** (c) **Nose** (d) **Undercarriage**

9 Making fresh water from salt is called… what?
(a) **Mineralisation** (b) **Desalination** (c) **Dehydration** (d) **Vaccination**

10 Crabeater, leopard and grey are all kinds of which animal?
(a) **Whale** (b) **Seal** (c) **Gull** (d) **Cat**

Quiz 17 score

General Knowledge QUIZ

18

Q4

1 What's the capital of Norway?
(a) **Helsinki**   (b) **Monaco**   (c) **Oslo**   (d) **Berlin**

2 Which of these languages is not spoken in India?
(a) **Hindi**   (b) **Bengali**   (c) **Urdu**   (d) **Javanese**

3 Reagan, Nixon and Clinton were all American… what?
(a) **Film stars**   (b) **Pop bands**   (c) **Presidents**   (d) **Baseball stars**

4 The home of an otter:
(a) **Lair**   (b) **Nest**   (c) **Eyrie**   (d) **Holt**

Q7

5 In which ocean are the Solomon Islands?
(a) **Pacific**   (b) **Indian**   (c) **Atlantic**   (d) **Arctic**

6 How many years is a silver wedding anniversary?
(a) **10**   (b) **15**   (c) **25**   (d) **50**

7 Who was the first Roman emperor?
(a) **Julius Caesar**   (b) **Mark Antony**   (c) **Nero**   (d) **Augustus**

8 Who was the first European to see the Pacific Ocean?
(a) **Balboa**   (b) **Columbus**   (c) **Drake**   (d) **Cook**

9 The grub of an insect is its… what?
(a) **Lava**   (b) **Guava**   (c) **Cuticle**   (d) **Larva**

10 Which is the largest of these islands?
(a) **Wight**   (b) **Greenland**   (c) **Madagascar**   (d) **Ireland**

Q9

Quiz 18 score

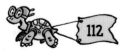

General Knowledge QUIZ

19

Q1

Q4

1. Which of these animals is the fastest runner?
   (a) **Lion**   (b) **Zebra**   (c) **Rabbit**   (d) **Cheetah**

2. In which mountains is the country of Andorra?
   (a) **Himalayas**   (b) **Alps**   (c) **Andes**   (d) **Pyrenees**

3. How many years are in a millennium?
   (a) **10**   (b) **100**   (c) **1000**   (d) **10,000**

4. An animal known for its sting in the tail:
   (a) **Skunk**   (b) **Spider**   (c) **Scorpion**   (d) **Wombat**

5. What is K2, a landmark in Asia?
   (a) **A road**   (b) **A mountain**   (c) **A river**   (d) **A tower**

6. Which is not a snake?
   (a) **Viper**   (b) **Anaconda**   (c) **Boa**   (d) **Cayman**

7. Which is not true of light?
   (a) **Makes a shadow**   (b) **Travels in straight lines**
   (c) **Passes through wood**   (d) **Travels very fast**

8. Who never ruled Russia?
   (a) **Ivan**   (b) **Catherine**   (c) **Basil**   (d) **Louis**

Q9

9. Which country's capital is Wellington?
   (a) **Australia**   (b) **New Zealand**   (c) **Zambia**   (d) **South Africa**

10. What kind of animals are Friesians?
    (a) **Cattle**   (b) **Pigs**   (c) **Sheep**   (d) **Cats**

Quiz 19 score

113

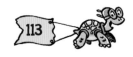

General Knowledge QUIZ

20

Q1

 1 Which countries fought the Punic Wars?
(a) **Rome v. Carthage**   (b) **Greeks v. Persians**   (c) **Celts v. Romans**
(d) **English v. Scots**

 2 When are nocturnal animals most lively?
(a) **Winter**   (b) **Night**   (c) **Day**   (d) **Rainy days**

 3 In which country are Dusseldorf and Frankfurt?
(a) **Germany**   (b) **France**   (c) **Italy**   (d) **Sweden**

Q10

 4 What colour is the cross on Finland's flag?
(a) **Green**   (b) **Blue**   (c) **Red**   (d) **White**

 5 Who is the patron saint of Ireland?
(a) **David**   (b) **Denis**   (c) **George**   (d) **Patrick**

 6 What's the nut of an oak tree?
(a) **Cob nut**   (b) **Acorn**   (c) **Catkin**   (d) **Chestnut**

Q4

 7 Which is not a lake?
(a) **Amazon**   (b) **Huron**   (c) **Superior**   (d) **Victoria**

 8 What do we call the envelope of gas around the Earth?
(a) **Crust**   (b) **Space**   (c) **Universe**   (d) **Atmosphere**

 9 Where were the ancient Hanging Gardens?
(a) **Olympia**   (b) **Ephesus**   (c) **Rhodes**   (d) **Babylon**

 10 The remains of an animal preserved in rock are called... what?
(a) **Relic**   (b) **Fossil**   (c) **Grave**   (d) **Embryo**

Quiz 20 score

General Knowledge QUIZ

21

Q5

		Your answer	Book answer

1. Who was not a US president?
   (a) **Lincoln** (b) **Nottingham** (c) **Hoover** (d) **Clinton**

Q3

2. Runner, haricot and French are all varieties of which vegetable?
   (a) **Carrots** (b) **Potatoes** (c) **Peas** (d) **Beans**

3. Where do black swans come from originally?
   (a) **Africa** (b) **China** (c) **India** (d) **Australia**

4. The maple leaf is the symbol of which country?
   (a) **Canada** (b) **New Zealand** (c) **Italy** (d) **Pakistan**

5. Who might experience 7gs?
   (a) **Rock singer** (b) **Climber** (c) **Astronaut** (d) **Miner**

6. Which country has the biggest population?
   (a) **India** (b) **USA** (c) **China** (d) **Russia**

7. At which soccer match does the crowd see most goals?
   (a) **4–4** (b) **6–3** (c) **3–7** (d) **7–2**

Q8

8. How many laps does a 5000 m runner complete on the track?
   (a) **4** (b) **12** (c) **20** (d) **30**

9. What kind of animal was the extinct Mastodon?
   (a) **Elephant** (b) **Bear** (c) **Dinosaur** (d) **Whale**

10. Which word describes the brightness of a star?
    (a) **Magnetism** (b) **Boldness** (c) **Magnitude** (d) **Shinyness**

Quiz 21 score

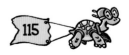

General Knowledge QUIZ

22

Q7

 1 Spell the composer:
(a) **Mostart** (b) **Mozart** (c) **Motsart** (d) **Motson**

 2 What's the square root of 121?
(a) **11** (b) **10** (c) **9** (d) **12**

Q5

 3 Spell the capital of China:
(a) **Baking** (b) **Beijing** (c) **Berlin** (d) **Benin**

 4 Which word means 'a scented ball'?
(a) **Pomander** (b) **Pergola** (c) **Pomegranate** (d) **Colander**

 5 Where might you find an 'apse'?
(a) **Zoo** (b) **Supermarket** (c) **Church** (d) **Submarine**

 6 Who might have 'green fingers'?
(a) **An alien** (b) **A chef** (c) **A cricketer** (d) **A gardener**

 7 Unjumble the letters to make an animal:
(a) **TOAG** (b) **IHARC** (c) **ENP** (d) **KOOB**

 8 What colour is azure?
(a) **Green** (b) **Blue** (c) **Black** (d) **Red**

 9 Roughly how high is Mount Everest?
(a) **1000 m** (b) **3000 m** (c) **5000 m** (d) **8000 m**

Q6

 10 Which word means 'very pleased'?
(a) **Dismayed** (b) **Dejected** (c) **Despondent** (d) **Delighted**

Quiz 22 score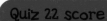

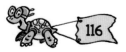

General Knowledge
QUIZ
23

Q10

Q2

 1 Which is not something to eat?
(a) **Risotto** (b) **Chowder** (c) **Biryani** (d) **Detergent**

 2 What's the collective name for a lot of bees?
(a) **Nest** (b) **Brood** (c) **Swarm** (d) **Gathering**

 3 In what language is 'she' elle ?
(a) **French** (b) **German** (c) **Italian** (d) **Spanish**

 4 Which is not a female?
(a) **Empress** (b) **Princess** (c) **Sultan** (d) **Duchess**

 5 Who wrote *Pride and Prejudice*?
(a) **Charles Dickens** (b) **Jane Austen** (c) **George Eliot**
(d) **Rudyard Kipling**

 6 How many thirds in 9 wholes?
(a) **20** (b) **18** (c) **27** (d) **36**

Q4

 7 What is 10 to 4 in the morning on a 24-hour clock?
(a) **03.50** (b) **04.10** (c) **15.50** (d) **4.45**

 8 Who was Queen Victoria's husband?
(a) **Algernon** (b) **Albert** (c) **Alfred** (d) **Aloysius**

 9 Which of these is not a river?
(a) **Shannon** (b) **Clyde** (c) **Windermere** (d) **Mersey**

 10 Which dog is German?
(a) **Chow** (b) **Saluki** (c) **Poodle** (d) **Dachshund**

Quiz 23 score

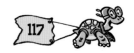

General Knowledge QUIZ

24

Your answer | Book answer

1 Which is a tool for making holes?
(a) **Punch** (b) **Pincers** (c) **Vice** (d) **Plane**

2 What would you do with semaphore?
(a) **Eat it** (b) **Send messages** (c) **Wear it** (d) **Bury it**

3 How many letters are there in the alphabet?
(a) **15** (b) **22** (c) **24** (d) **26**

Q7

4 Which city goes with sprouts (the vegetable)?
(a) **Bruges** (b) **Birmingham** (c) **Brussels** (d) **Berlin**

5 Which food is German in origin?
(a) **Burger** (b) **Pizza** (c) **Curry** (d) **Sushi**

6 To which family do crabs belong?
(a) **Crustaceans** (b) **Amphibians** (c) **Bacteria** (d) **Dinosaurs**

7 Which of these would fire a bow and arrow?
(a) **Lurcher** (b) **Archer** (c) **Halberdier** (d) **Fletcher**

8 What would a cook use to separate the lumps from flour?
(a) **Sieve** (b) **Skillet** (c) **Slice** (d) **Spatula**

Q6

9 Which is a dangerous chemical insecticide?
(a) **MOT** (b) **TNT** (c) **DDT** (d) **SST**

10 In which city are the UN Headquarters?
(a) **Moscow** (b) **Paris** (c) **London** (d) **New York**

Quiz 24 score

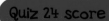

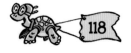

General Knowledge QUIZ

25

Q10

1 Which is not a conifer tree?
(a) **Larch** (b) **Spruce** (c) **Pine** (d) **Oak**

Q8

2 How many states are there in the USA?
(a) **35** (b) **40** (c) **48** (d) **50**

3 Which of these is a Hindu festival?
(a) **Diwali** (b) **Ramadan** (c) **Purim** (d) **Easter**

4 Which animal has a fleece?
(a) **Wolf** (b) **Sheep** (c) **Stoat** (d) **Horse**

5 What's the opposite of mortal?
(a) **Unmortal** (b) **Infinite** (c) **Immortal** (d) **Dead**

6 Which king won the battle of Agincourt?
(a) **Louis XII** (b) **Henry I** (c) **Henry V** (d) **John**

7 What's the capital of Australia?
(a) **Darwin** (b) **Sydney** (c) **Melbourne** (d) **Canberra**

8 Which explorer reached the South Pole in 1911?
(a) **Livingstone** (b) **Peary** (c) **Amundsen** (d) **Franklin**

Q4

9 An international cricket or rugby match is called a... what?
(a) **Trial** (b) **Test** (c) **Challenge** (d) **Showdown**

10 Which puppet character has a wife named Judy?
(a) **Pinocchio** (b) **Punch** (c) **Sooty** (d) **Brains**

Quiz 25 score

General Knowledge QUIZ

26

Q9

		Your answer	Book answer

1 Who wrote *The Jungle Book*?
(a) **Tarzan** (b) **Kipling** (c) **Scott** (d) **Fleming**

2 Which painter went off to live in the south seas?
(a) **Gauguin** (b) **Constable** (c) **Michelangelo** (d) **Picasso**

Q10

3 Which Derbyshire town is famous for its tarts?
(a) **Sandwich** (b) **Bakewell** (c) **Melton Mowbray** (d) **Eccles**

4 Which is a variety of apple?
(a) **Bramley** (b) **Jaffa** (c) **Cos** (d) **King Edward**

5 Style of music made popular by Bob Marley:
(a) **Country and western** (b) **Reggae** (c) **Bebop** (d) **Swing**

6 Which animal was the first ever astronaut?
(a) **A monkey** (b) **A cat** (c) **A frog** (d) **A dog**

7 What's the longest river in South America?
(a) **Volga** (b) **Amazon** (c) **Congo** (d) **Rio Grande**

8 On which date were the D-Day landings in 1944?
(a) **25 December** (b) **8 August** (c) **1 May** (d) **6 June**

9 Which bird has the longest tail feathers?
(a) **Bird of Paradise** (b) **Eagle** (c) **Albatross** (d) **Macaw**

Q5

10 Which is not a member of the dog family?
(a) **Coyote** (b) **Dingo** (c) **Jackal** (d) **Wombat**

Quiz 26 score

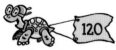

General Knowledge QUIZ

27

Q4

Your answer
Book answer

1 Which motorway links the English Midlands to the West Country?
(a) **M5**   (b) **M2**   (c) **M8**   (d) **M25**

2 Spell the bubbly French drink:
(a) **Shampane**   (b) **Champagne**   (c) **Shampayne**   (d) **Champain**

Q7

3 Who was the Saxon who fought the Normans?
(a) **Cnut**   (b) **Hereward**   (c) **William Wallace**   (d) **Boudicca**

4 Which is a large heavy water snake?
(a) **Cobra**   (b) **Anaconda**   (c) **Manatee**   (d) **Rattlesnake**

5 Which name describes someone or something very large?
(a) **Goliath**   (b) **Prima donna**   (c) **Supremo**   (d) **Maestro**

6 Which was worn on the head?   Q6
(a) **Breeches**   (b) **Bonnet**   (c) **Doublet**   (d) **Waistcoat**

7 Who was the notorious pirate?
(a) **Blackbeard**   (b) **Bluebeard**   (c) **Rednose**   (d) **Bigears**

8 Spell the south American country:
(a) **Youragguay**   (b) **Urugooay**   (c) **Uruguay**   (d) **Oooergway**

9 How many categories are there in the Dewey Decimal System?
(a) **2**   (b) **5**   (c) **10**   (d) **20**

10 What's the name of the latest and biggest 'Queen' cruise liner?
(a) **Queen Elizabeth 2**   (b) **Queen Victoria**   (c) **Queen Mother**
(d) **Queen Mary 2**

Quiz 27 score

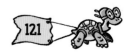

121

General Knowledge QUIZ

28

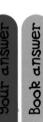

Q3

 1 Which was never part of the British Empire, though in the Commonwealth now?
(a) **Canada**   (b) **Sri Lanka**   (c) **Jamaica**   (d) **Mozambique**

 2 Which is not a musical instrument?
(a) **Oboe**   (b) **Hobo**   (c) **Bassoon**   (d) **Recorder**

 3 Who invaded Britain in AD43?
(a) **Celts**   (b) **Romans**   (c) **Saxons**   (d) **Normans**

Q4

 4 Which animal lives in a lodge?
(a) **Beaver**   (b) **Otter**   (c) **Fox**   (d) **Bear**

 5 What is the currency in Ireland?
(a) **Punt**   (b) **Euro**   (c) **Dollar**   (d) **Mark**

 6 In which city does the Scottish Parliament meet?
(a) **Perth**   (b) **Glasgow**   (c) **St Andrews**   (d) **Edinburgh**

 7 In what year did Queen Victoria die?   Q10
(a) **1901**   (b) **1837**   (c) **1926**   (d) **1939**

 8 Who was not Prime Minister in wartime Britain (1939–45)?
(a) **Eden**   (b) **Chamberlain**   (c) **Churchill**   (d) **Attlee**

 9 Which bird is being reintroduced to England?
(a) **Marabou stork**   (b) **Great bustard**   (c) **Vulture**   (d) **Secretary bird**

 10 What was a medieval basinet?
(a) **Knight's helmet**   (b) **Monk's washing up bowl**   (c) **Castle toilet**
(d) **Guitar**

Quiz 28 score

Chart Your Scores

	1	2	3	4	5	6	7	8	9	10
Quiz 1										
Quiz 2										
Quiz 3										
Quiz 4										
Quiz 5										
Quiz 6										
Quiz 7										
Quiz 8										
Quiz 9										
Quiz 10										
Quiz 11										
Quiz 12										
Quiz 13										
Quiz 14										
Quiz 15										
Quiz 16										
Quiz 17										
Quiz 18										
Quiz 19										
Quiz 20										
Quiz 21										
Quiz 22										
Quiz 23										
Quiz 24										
Quiz 25										
Quiz 26										
Quiz 27										
Quiz 28										

Words and Writing Answers

Quiz 1
1b, 2b, 3c, 4a, 5c, 6d, 7a, 8b, 9b, 10c

Quiz 2
1b, 2d, 3a, 4b, 5a, 6a, 7d, 8c, 9b, 10d

Quiz 3
1a, 2c, 3b, 4d, 5d, 6d, 7b, 8c, 9b, 10c

Quiz 4
1b, 2c, 3a, 4d, 5b, 6b, 7a, 8a, 9c, 10b

Quiz 5
1c, 2c, 3c, 4a, 5b, 6a, 7c, 8a, 9b, 10a

Quiz 6
1b, 2b, 3b, 4b, 5a, 6a, 7a, 8a, 9b, 10c

Quiz 7
1a, 2d, 3b, 4c, 5a, 6b, 7d, 8c, 9a, 10a

Quiz 8
1c, 2d, 3a, 4b, 5a, 6c, 7b, 8c, 9a, 10c

Quiz 9
1d, 2a, 3b, 4b, 5b, 6c, 7a, 8c, 9d, 10a

Quiz 10
1a, 2c, 3b, 4a, 5c, 6d, 7b, 8d, 9a, 10d

Quiz 11
1b, 2c, 3d, 4a, 5a, 6d, 7c, 8a, 9b, 10a

Quiz 12
1b, 2a, 3d, 4a, 5d, 6b, 7b, 8b, 9c, 10b

Quiz 13
1b, 2c, 3c, 4c, 5b, 6a, 7d, 8b, 9d, 10c

Quiz 14
1d, 2a, 3d, 4a, 5b, 6d, 7d, 8d, 9c, 10b

Quiz 15
1a, 2b, 3d, 4a, 5b, 6c, 7a, 8c, 9c, 10d

Quiz 16
1b, 2c, 3c, 4d, 5a, 6d, 7d, 8a, 9b, 10d

Quiz 17
1a, 2c, 3c, 4a, 5b, 6a, 7c, 8b, 9d, 10b

Quiz 18
1a, 2b, 3c, 4d, 5a, 6b, 7b, 8b, 9b, 10c

Quiz 19
1b, 2d, 3a, 4b, 5a, 6d, 7b, 8b, 9a, 10c

Quiz 20
1c, 2b, 3d, 4d, 5c, 6a, 7b, 8a, 9a, 10d

Quiz 21
1b, 2a, 3c, 4a, 5c, 6d, 7b, 8a, 9b, 10d

Quiz 22
1b, 2a, 3a, 4b, 5c, 6a, 7d, 8b, 9b, 10b

Quiz 23
1c, 2d, 3b, 4a, 5b, 6c, 7a, 8d, 9a, 10c

Quiz 24
1a, 2c, 3c, 4b, 5a, 6a, 7b, 8b, 9a, 10c

Quiz 25
1a, 2c, 3c, 4c, 5b, 6a, 7a, 8b, 9b, 10c

Quiz 26
1a, 2d, 3a, 4b, 5d, 6d, 7d, 8a, 9a, 10c

Quiz 27
1d, 2c, 3a, 4a, 5d, 6a, 7a, 8b, 9d, 10c

Quiz 28
1c, 2b, 3b, 4a, 5a, 6b, 7c, 8d, 9d, 10a

Using Numbers Answers

Quiz 1
1b, 2c, 3a, 4b, 5b, 6c, 7a, 8b, 9a, 10c

Quiz 2
1a, 2b, 3c, 4a, 5b, 6d, 7b, 8d, 9a, 10d

Quiz 3
1c, 2b, 3d, 4b, 5c, 6b, 7d, 8c, 9a, 10d

Quiz 4
1d, 2a, 3b, 4d, 5a, 6b, 7d, 8b, 9c, 10a

Quiz 5
1c, 2c, 3b, 4c, 5d, 6a, 7a, 8b, 9d, 10a

Quiz 6
1a, 2c, 3b, 4a, 5a, 6c, 7a, 8b, 9c, 10a

Quiz 7
1a, 2b, 3d, 4c, 5a, 6b, 7a, 8d, 9d, 10d

Quiz 8
1a, 2d, 3b, 4c, 5a, 6c, 7d, 8a, 9c, 10b

Quiz 9
1a, 2c, 3b, 4b, 5c, 6c, 7b, 8b, 9d, 10a

Quiz 10
1b, 2b, 3c, 4d, 5a, 6d, 7c, 8a, 9c, 10c

Quiz 11
1c, 2a, 3b, 4b, 5b, 6d, 7c, 8c, 9b, 10b

Quiz 12
1b, 2c, 3d, 4b, 5a, 6a, 7a, 8d, 9b, 10b

Quiz 13
1c, 2b, 3a, 4c, 5a, 6b, 7b, 8b, 9a, 10d

Quiz 14
1b, 2c, 3a, 4d, 5a, 6b, 7d, 8d, 9b, 10a

Quiz 15
1d, 2b, 3b, 4c, 5a, 6b, 7d, 8b, 9b, 10c

Quiz 16
1b. 2c, 3a, 4d, 5b, 6d, 7c, 8b, 9a, 10d

Quiz 17
1a, 2b, 3d, 4a, 5c, 6c, 7b, 8d, 9d, 10a

Quiz 18
1b, 2c, 3d, 4b, 5c, 6d, 7a, 8b, 9b, 10a

Quiz 19
1d, 2b, 3b, 4a, 5c, 6a, 7b, 8c, 9b, 10d

Quiz 20
1d, 2d, 3b, 4c, 5c, 6b, 7d, 8c, 9d, 10b

Quiz 21
1c, 2d, 3d, 4d, 5d, 6c, 7b, 8b, 9b, 10a

Quiz 22
1c, 2a, 3c, 4d, 5c, 6b, 7c, 8c, 9c, 10c

Quiz 23
1a, 2c, 3d, 4b, 5b, 6c, 7c, 8b, 9c, 10c

Quiz 24
1a, 2c, 3d, 4c, 5b, 6c, 7b, 8b, 9d, 10d

Quiz 25
1d, 2b, 3c, 4b, 5c, 6c, 7d, 8c, 9c, 10c

Quiz 26
1c, 2a, 3d, 4c, 5c, 6a, 7b, 8b, 9d, 10c

Quiz 27
1d, 2b, 3b, 4d, 5c, 6b, 7d, 8c, 9c, 10d

Quiz 28
1c, 2a, 3b, 4c, 5b, 6c, 7c, 8a, 9d, 10d

Everyday Science Answers

Quiz 1
1d, 2d, 3a, 4a, 5d, 6a, 7c, 8c, 9a, 10d

Quiz 2
1c, 2a, 3b, 4b, 5a, 6d, 7a, 8c, 9b, 10c

Quiz 3
1a, 2a, 3c, 4b, 5b, 6c, 7d, 8a, 9b, 10b

Quiz 4
1c, 2a, 3c, 4d, 5c, 6c, 7b, 8a, 9c, 10a

Quiz 5
1b, 2a, 3a, 4d, 5b, 6c, 7a, 8c, 9c, 10d

Quiz 6
1d, 2a, 3d, 4b, 5c, 6a, 7b, 8c, 9a, 10c

Quiz 7
1d, 2b, 3b, 4c, 5c, 6b, 7c, 8b, 9b, 10d

Quiz 8
1c, 2a, 3d, 4b, 5d, 6a, 7b, 8c, 9b, 10b

Quiz 9
1b, 2c, 3a, 4a, 5b, 6a, 7d, 8c, 9a, 10c

Quiz 10
1b, 2d, 3a, 4c, 5b, 6b, 7a, 8d, 9d, 10b

Quiz 11
1b, 2d, 3c, 4d, 5c, 6b, 7a, 8c, 9b, 10a

Quiz 12
1c, 2a, 3b, 4d, 5a, 6a, 7b, 8b, 9a, 10d

Quiz 13
1a, 2a, 3d, 4b, 5a, 6d, 7d, 8a, 9a, 10b

Quiz 14
1b, 2c, 3a, 4c, 5c, 6b, 7b, 8b, 9a, 10c

Quiz 15
1a, 2b, 3d, 4d, 5c, 6d, 7a, 8d, 9b, 10c

Quiz 16
1c, 2a, 3c, 4d, 5a, 6a, 7b, 8b, 9c, 10a

Quiz 17
1c, 2c, 3b, 4d, 5c, 6b, 7c, 8d, 9a, 10c

Quiz 18
1a, 2a, 3d, 4a, 5b, 6a, 7b, 8b, 9a, 10d

Quiz 19
1b, 2b, 3a, 4d, 5c, 6b, 7a, 8b, 9b, 10b

Quiz 20
1a, 2b, 3a, 4b, 5b, 6b, 7d, 8a, 9c, 10b

Quiz 21
1c, 2a, 3c, 4a, 5c, 6b, 7d, 8a, 9b, 10a

Quiz 22
1c, 2d, 3a, 4b, 5c, 6b, 7b, 8a, 9b, 10c

Quiz 23
1b, 2a, 3d, 4b, 5d, 6a, 7b, 8c, 9a, 10a

Quiz 24
1b, 2d, 3b, 4a, 5a, 6d, 7c, 8b, 9a, 10c

Quiz 25
1d, 2b, 3b, 4a, 5a, 6b, 7d, 8c, 9b, 10d

Quiz 26
1c, 2d, 3c, 4a, 5c, 6a, 7b, 8c, 9b, 10c

Quiz 27
1b, 2b, 3d, 4a, 5c, 6d, 7a, 8d, 9c, 10b

Quiz 28
1b, 2b, 3d, 4d, 5a, 6b, 7c, 8a, 9c, 10b

General Knowledge Answers

Quiz 1
1a, 2a, 3a, 4a, 5d, 6c, 7a, 8c, 9b, 10d

Quiz 2
1d, 2c, 3d, 4c, 5b, 6a, 7a, 8d, 9d, 10a

Quiz 3
1a, 2b, 3d, 4b, 5c, 6d, 7d, 8a, 9c, 10a

Quiz 4
1a, 2d, 3a, 4c, 5b, 6a, 7a, 8c, 9a, 10a

Quiz 5
1b, 2a, 3c, 4b, 5d, 6a, 7d, 8a, 9b, 10c

Quiz 6
1a, 2b, 3a, 4b, 5a, 6d, 7c, 8c, 9a, 10d

Quiz 7
1d, 2b, 3b, 4a, 5a, 6b, 7a, 8d, 9a, 10c

Quiz 8
1c, 2a, 3c, 4c, 5d, 6b, 7c, 8b, 9b, 10c

Quiz 9
1a, 2d, 3b, 4c, 5c, 6a, 7a, 8d, 9a, 10c

Quiz 10
1a, 2c, 3d, 4d, 5b, 6b, 7b, 8d, 9b, 10a

Quiz 11
1c, 2a, 3d, 4a, 5b, 6d, 7d, 8a, 9a, 10b

Quiz 12
1a, 2c, 3a, 4a, 5c, 6c, 7c, 8b, 9a, 10b

Quiz 13
1a, 2d, 3d, 4a, 5d, 6d, 7b, 8d, 9a, 10c

Quiz 14
1c, 2a, 3a, 4b, 5c, 6c, 7a, 8b, 9b, 10c

Quiz 15
1a, 2b, 3d, 4b, 5b, 6d, 7b, 8a, 9b, 10d

Quiz 16
1c, 2d, 3c, 4a, 5c, 6b, 7b, 8d, 9c, 10d

Quiz 17
1a, 2c, 3c, 4d, 5a, 6d, 7c, 8a, 9b, 10b

Quiz 18
1c, 2d, 3c, 4d, 5a, 6c, 7d, 8a, 9d, 10b

Quiz 19
1d, 2d, 3c, 4c, 5b, 6d, 7c, 8d, 9b, 10a

Quiz 20
1a, 2b, 3a, 4b, 5d, 6b, 7a, 8d, 9d, 10b

Quiz 21
1b, 2d, 3d, 4a, 5c, 6c, 7c, 8b, 9a, 10c

Quiz 22
1b, 2a, 3b, 4a, 5c, 6d, 7a, 8b, 9d, 10d

Quiz 23
1d, 2c, 3a, 4c, 5b, 6c, 7a, 8b, 9c, 10d

Quiz 24
1a, 2b, 3d, 4c, 5a, 6a, 7b, 8a, 9c, 10d

Quiz 25
1d, 2d, 3a, 4b, 5c, 6c, 7d, 8c, 9b, 10b

Quiz 26
1b, 2a, 3b, 4a, 5b, 6d, 7b, 8d, 9a, 10d

Quiz 27
1a, 2b, 3b, 4b, 5a, 6b, 7a, 8c, 9c, 10d

Quiz 28
1a, 2b, 3b, 4a, 5b, 6d, 7a, 8a, 9b, 10a